Kyoto University African Study Series 031

Tera Askebari
Ethnography of Transport Workers in Addis Ababa

Eunji Choi

Center for African Area Studies, Kyoto University
Yoshida-Shimoadachi-cho 46, Sakyo, Kyoto 606-8501

First Published 2023 by Shoukadoh Book Sellers

Library of Congress Cataloguing-in-Publication-Data

Choi Eunji
Tera Askebari Ethnography of Transport Workers in Addis Ababa
ISBN978-4-87974-789-1

This book was published with supports of Center for African Area Studies,
Kyoto University.

Contents

List of Tables

List of Figures

List of Acronyms

AACPPO	Addis Ababa City Planning Project Office
AACCSA	Addis Ababa Chamber of Commerce and Sectoral Associations
AAMSEDB	Addis Ababa Micro and Small Enterprise Development Bureau
AARTB	Addis Ababa Road and Transport Bureau
ACBE	Anbessa City Bus Service Enterprise
BRT	Bus Rapid Transit
CITAO	Compagnia Italiana Transporti Africa Orientale
CSA	Central Statistical Agency
CUD	Coalition for Unity and Democracy
EDRP	Emergency Demobilization and Reintegration Project
EPRDF	Ethiopian People's Revolutionary Democratic Front
FeMSEDA	Federal Micro and Small Enterprises Development Agency
FTA	Federal Transport Authority
IEG	Independent Evaluation Group
ILO	International Labour Organization
MSEs	Micro and Small Enterprises
ReMSEDAs	Regional Micro and Small Enterprises Development Agencies
UN	United Nations
UNDESA	United Nations Department of Economic and Social Affair

Notation

Amharic is a language which is consisted with 33 basic consonants and 7 basic vowels, having about 290 sounds. The Amharic script is called *fidel* (ፊደል), and each *fidel* are representing one sound. Due to its richness on the types of sounds, there were some limitations to write some sounds into roman characters. Thus, I tried to use roman alphabet that is similar to the original sound.

The local terms are written in roman alphabet with the *italic* letters. Additionally, I put the *fidel* alphabets in brackets next to each term. The local terms that are written in this thesis are refer to the chart below.

List of Vowels

Fidel	Pronunciation	*Roman alphabet*
አ	ä	*e*
ኡ	u	*u*
ኢ	i	*i*
ኣ	a	*a*
ኤ	e	*e*
እ	ə	*e*
ኦ	o	*o*

List of Consonants

Fidel (first order)	Pronunciation	*Roman alphabet*	*Fidel* (first order)	Pronunc-iation	*Roman alphabet*
ሀ	/h/	*h*	ከ	/k/	*k*
ለ	/l/	*l*	ኸ	/x/ or h	*h*
ሐ	/h/	*h*	ወ	/w/	*w*
መ	/m/	*m*	ዐ	'	*a*
ሠ	/s/	*s*	ዘ	/z/	*z*
ረ	/r/	*r*	ዠ	/ʒ/ or ž	*zy*
ሰ	/s/	*s*	የ	/j/ or y	*y*

ሸ	/ʃ/ or š	sh	ደ	/d/	d
ቀ	/k'/	k'	ጀ	/dʒ/ or ğ	j
በ	/b/	b	ገ	/g/	g
ቨ	/β/ or v	v	ጠ	/t'/	t'
ተ	/t/	t	ጨ	/tʃ/ or č	ch'
ቸ	/tʃ/ or č	ch	ጰ	/p'/	p'
ኀ	/h/	h	ጸ	/ts'/ or ṣ	ts'
ነ	/n/	n	ፀ	/ts'/ or ṣ	ts'
ኘ	/ɲ/ or ň	ny	ፈ	/f/	f
አ	'	a	ፐ	/p/	p

Chapter 1. Introduction

Background of the study

Car Rapide in Senegal, *Matatu* in Kenya, *Tro-tro* in Ghana, and minibus (locally called *taxi*) in Addis Ababa. All of these are paratransit services operating in Africa, which refers to small bus or minibus services that operate privately and without a fixed schedule. Since the 1980s, African cities have experienced a high degree of urbanization, and providing equitable mobility services has become more important than ever. This led to the rise of paratransit service, in the void of government-owned public transports. Currently, they deliver about 70 to 90% of urban mobility in African cities (Howe & Bryceson 2000: 37; Venter et al. 2007: 662).

Despite the crucial role that they deliver, transport workers' activities have been largely perceived negatively, as flouting the traffic regulation, unmethodical practice, or collecting excessive fares were common phenomena (Gleave et al. 2005: 121; Mintesnot & Takano 2007: 31). It was also common to observe them affronting the passengers or collect excessive fares. Thus, transport workers in Africa were largely portrayed as violent, thuggish, or aggressive men in various literatures (Kenda 2006; Emmanuel 2015: 94-106). While some see this as a personal trait (Fekadu 2014: 124-125), various external factors such as exploitative income structure, the struggle for survival, and passengers' pressing are influencing and causing reproduction of in/formalities in this industry (for example, Rizzo 2011). In these circumstances, the distinction between the outlaw and the queue keeper is often blurred, and transport workers' "informalities" has become the norm in this industry.

In Addis Ababa, the minibus is the most commonly used transport service. Approximately 20,000 minibuses operate daily, with passengers utilizing the minibus service accounts for 90% of total transport rates (Addis Ababa Road and Transport Bureau [AARTB] 2019). In the middle of this business, there are groups of people called *tera askebari*, who are controlling the flow of minibuses and passengers at minibus terminals. The *tera askebari* initially started their business informally, but most of the groups acquired a legal status after the intervention of the Micro and Small Enterprises Development Agency in 2011. Despite their shift to formal status, informal aspects were still remaining in their hiring practices and minibus management activities. Accordingly, the perception of the *tera askebari* has been largely negative, both socially and academically, and they are often underestimated as thugs who resort to street violence and utilize money for personal purposes (Addis Ababa Chamber of Commerce and Sectoral Associations [AACCSA] 2009: 178; Di Nunzio 2012: 440). Notwithstanding their crucial role, their activities have been frowned upon as being unmethodical, and attempts to determine their role and contribution in society have not been achieved.

Research site: Addis Ababa

Ethiopia is a country located in the northeastern part of Africa, in the center of the "Horn of Africa." This country shares a border with Sudan and South Sudan in the west, Kenya in the south, Somalia and Djibouti in the east and Eritrea in the north (Figure 1). It is the second-most populous country in Africa, with a population of over 115 million (World Bank 2022a). Ethiopia counts over 80 ethnic groups and 92 languages, and majorities are Afro-Asiatic language groups that are mainly Cushitic and Semitic, which include Amharic, Tigrinya, and Oromo. There are also Omotic languages which are concentrated in west Ethiopia and some Nilo-Saharan languages are found in the southwestern part of the country. Among many languages, Amharic and English are used as official working languages. The country shows huge diversity in altitude as well with the lowest point of the Danakil Depression in the Afar region, which is 125m below sea level and the highest point of Ras Dashen Mountain which reaches 4,550m. Politically, Ethiopia adopts ethnic federalism which gives each ethnic group the constitutional right to govern its own affairs (Aalen. 2011). This is reflected in the administrative units of the country, which are divided into 11 regional states represented by major ethnic groups, and two independent city administrations, that is Addis Ababa and Dire Dawa.

In this country of diversity, Addis Ababa serves as the capital city of Ethiopia. It is founded in 1889 by Emperor Menelik II, entitled by the name "new flower" in Amharic. Over the past years, Ethiopia has achieved a high level of economic development, achieving 9.8% of GDP growth in the past 10 years (2009 to 2018) while the world average remained 2.5% (World Bank 2021). This metropolitan city served as a robust engine for national development and worked as a main diplomatic player in Africa by operating various headquarters of international organizations such as the African Union, the United Nations Economic Commission for Africa, and about 115 embassies. Due to the rapid urbanization,

Addis Ababa is experiencing population growth, from 390,000 in 1950 has increased to 4,794,000 in 2020, and is expected to reach 9 million by 2035 (United Nation Department of Economic and Social Affairs [UNDESA] 2018).

Figure 1. Geographical location of Ethiopia (drawn by author)

Making cities in motion: Minibus and *tera askebari*

The development of the city has brought the increase in public transportation sector. As the city developed, the population increased dramatically and the growing population has led to an increased need for transportation. Nevertheless, the car ownership remained low, with only two people owning personal vehicles per 1,000 people, which is the lowest car ownership in Africa (Addis Ababa City Administration [AACA] 2011; International Organization of Motor Vehicle Manufacturers [OICA] 2021). It is largely due to the high rate of automotive tax which ranges from 132 per cent to 256 per cent, and due to this reason, most of the citizens had to rely their travel on public transportation and their high demands led to a diversification of the public transport services.

Demand for public transport has been met by minibuses (12—14-seat Toyota Hi-Ace bongo buses), which provide accessible and rapid services (Fekadu 2014: 125). The minibus is the major mode of transportation used by Addis Ababa citizens. It is locally called *taxi*, but in this study, I used the term "minibus" to differentiate it from the four-wheel taxicab service. The minibus service began in the late 1980s in the *Derg* socialist regime. Since its creation, the minibus industry has developed to correspond to the increasing mobility demand due to population growth (refer to UNDESA 2018). Table 1 presents the number of registered minibuses from 1999 to 2005 and in 2019. From 1999 to 2005, the number of vehicles increased gradually from 8,266 to 11,806. The number of minibuses reached 18,681 in 2019, reflecting approximately twofold growth versus 1999. Currently, approximately 20,000 minibuses operate daily in 239 routes at 150 terminals, with passengers utilizing the minibus service accounting for 90% of total transport rates (AARTB 2012; Frehiwot 2013: 12).

Table 1. Number of registered minibuses from 1999 to 2005 and in 2019 in Addis Ababa

Year	Number of fleets
1999 to 2000 (E.C.* 1992)	8,266
2000 to 2001 (E.C. 1993)	8,847
2001 to 2002 (E.C. 1994)	9,910
2002 to 2003 (E.C. 1995)	9,930
2003 to 2004 (E.C. 1996)	9,262
2004 to 2005 (E.C. 1997)	11,806
2019	18,681

Note: Data collected from Mintesnot & Takano (2007) and AARTB (2019).
* E.C.: Ethiopian Calendar

Figure 2. *Tera askebari* **at Arat Kilo Terminal**

In the middle of this business, there are groups of people called *tera askebari*, who are controlling the flow of minibuses and passengers at minibus terminals (Figure 2). *Tera* (ተራ) means queue and *askebari* (አስከባሪ) means someone who enforces or uphold something.[1] Thus, *tera askebari* (ተራ አስከባሪ) refer to a queue keeper who uphold certain rules. Of the various classes of *tera askebari*, my focus is confined to *tera askebari* who work on public transport sector, especially minibus.[2] Their major role is to keep the order of the minibuses and passengers at minibus terminals, but they also undertake social activities such as assisting the passengers and policing the surroundings at the terminal. Many of them are wearing work uniform with blue-white color, which is provided from the district police station, or fluorescent colored vest, which are sponsored by shopping malls or stores that are located closed to the minibus terminal. They collect tolls from minibuses every time they visit the terminal, from 2 up to 50 *birr*[3], depending on the length of the destination. Currently, there are approximately 138 individual *tera askebari* groups and 11,000 *tera askebari* working in about 150 minibus terminals in Addis Ababa.[4]

Objectives

Until now, the African transport sector has been understood as "informal" and treated as an underdeveloped sector that needs to be modernized. However, the distinction between the formal and the informal made it difficult to understand the heterogeneity of the transport sector, which is mixed with private and public, and formal and informal. Thus, understanding the "informality" should not simply be treated as the territory outside of formal regulation, however, investigating social background, actors' strategy and process of government intervention should be considered to fully understand its dynamics.

With the progress of urbanization and the rapid increase in people's mobility, much social and academic attention has been paid to minibuses in Addis Ababa, which account for more than 90% of the transport share. There is literature on traffic performance (Bayou 1991), methods on developing the transportation system (Mintesnot & Takano 2007), and various recommendations on improving traffic problems (Voukas & Palmer 2012; Berhanu 2017). There were also some studies of *tera askebari*, which mainly addressed on their relationship with the political interventions (Di Nunzio 2012, 2014, 2019). However, there is a lack of detailed research on the history of *tera askebari*, who share the minibus industry's development path.

This book is focused on the African transport workers' activity in how they survive and layout their livelihood strategies in the informal economy and shape the order of urban transport in Addis Ababa. In order to assert my argument, I use the term "formal" and "informal," which refers to economic activities inside and outside of the state regulatory boundary and try to shed light on their roles and livelihoods in the platform of urban transport in Africa. This thesis argues that *tera askebari* play a crucial role in the management of urban transportation in Addis Ababa, despite their activities showing some degree of flexibility.

In Amharic, a prefix *bale-* (ባለ-) means a master and *muya* (ሙያ) means skill. Thus, *balemuya* (ባለሙያ) has been traditionally meant a master-craftsman or experts, while it also refers to a person who is skilled and proficient in a certain field or activity. As an example, to explain what I experienced in Ethiopia, I was once called "*balemuya*" by my host family when I cooked delicious food. Thus, the usage of the terminology is not limited to the experts but is casually and widely used to refer to someone who performs a certain job or task. In this thesis, I argue that *tera askebari* are *balemuya*, smart strategists, who layout their livelihood strategies in the complex environment where formal and informal are exist, and shape the order of urban transport in Addis Ababa.

Methodology

Methodological approach

This study examines the activities of *tera askebari*. The major focus of our study is on the behavior of the *tera askebari* during minibus management, confrontations, and conversation in their daily lives. It also focuses on the micro-level interactions among the *tera askebari*, and their relations with minibus workers and public servants who represent the transport authority which regulate minibuses. Consequently, their relationship within the *tera askebari* community as well as their coping strategies were studied. To achieve a comprehensive understanding of these aspects, a combination of qualitative and quantitative methods is required.

Qualitative approaches are necessary to explore the *tera askebari*'s personal experiences, interpersonal relationships, and strategic behavior in managing minibuses. Observing the personal experiences and relationships of the *tera askebari* is essential to understand their motivations and the backgrounds of their management methods. Due to the absence of official guidelines in minibus management, the system is formulated through active interactions between the *tera askebari* and minibus workers. Thus, knowledge about informal factors such as personal experience, which reflect past events as well as their social network, is needed to determine the major factors that shape their management system. However, these aspects cannot be objectively measured. Thus, qualitative paradigms are better suited to study the experiences, relationships, and activities of the *tera askebari* in communicating with minibus-related actors.

On the other hand, quantitative approaches are more apt for identifying patterns in the *tera askebari*'s management of the minibuses. The *tera askebari*'s particular actions, the challenges they face, intervals between the departure of minibuses, and the relationship they have with minibus workers vary according to specific events and characteristics. These aspects of the study require a quantitative approach, especially the collection and analysis of aggregated datasets. Therefore, the mixed methods approach will be appropriate in this research because of the complex nature of the research questions. The combined methods of qualitative and quantitative approaches will allow for the development of a more complete understanding of the findings.

Methods and data collection process

The fieldwork was largely divided into two parts. First, to develop a general idea regarding the *tera askebari*, data were collected from multiple minibus terminals. After that, the research scope was narrowed down to specific terminal to observe the *tera askebari*'s activities intensively.

Since there was little literature related to the *tera askebari*, it was necessary to figure out their general characteristics and the background of their emergence. I used anthropological methodologies such as participant observation, in-depth interviews, and informal conversations with the *tera askebari*. The research was conducted in two phases, first, from June 21 to July 22, 2017, and then from July 7 to August 23, 2018. During the first research period, five interviews with the *tera askebari* were conducted. In the second period, in-depth interviews and small group discussions were conducted with the *tera askebari* at 27 minibus terminals (Figure 3 and Table 2). I collected data randomly, both in the center and in the outskirts of the city. The language that I used for the research was Amharic.

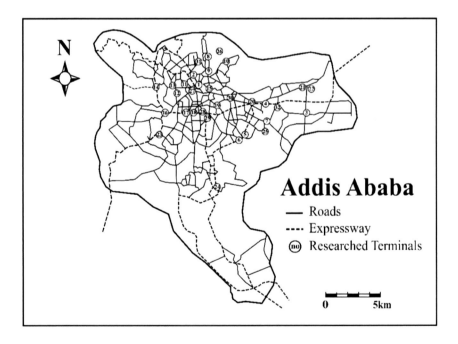

Figure 3. Map of research site in the first and second fieldwork

Table 2. List of *tera askebari* groups (terminals) that I researched

Group no.	Name of the terminals (Amharic alphabet)	Research period
1	Piazza (ፒያሳ)	2nd
2	Abune Petros (አቡነ ጴጥሮስ)	
3	Semit Condominium (ስሚት ኮንዶሚኒየም)	
4	Gurd Shola (ጉርድ ሾላ)	
5	Bole Bras (ቦሌ ብራስ)	1st
6	Bole (ቦሌ)	
7	Gerji Mabrat Hail (ገርጂ ማብራት ኃይል)	
8	Shiromeda (ሽሮሜዳ)	
9	Sidist Kilo (ስድስት ኪሎ)	
10	Faransai (ፈረንሳይ)	
11	Atikilt Tera (አትክልት ተራ)	
12	Marcato (መርካቶ)	
13	Autobus Tera (አውቶቡስ ተራ)	
14	Kolfe Keraniyo (ኮልፈ ቀራኒዮ)	
15	Arat Kilo (አራት ኪሎ)	
16	Ttorhailoch (ጦርኃይሎች)	
17	Mexico Square (ሜክሲኮ አደባባይ)	
18	Mexico Square - 2 (ሜክሲኮ አደባባይ)	
19	Kazanchis (ካዛንቺስ)	2nd
20	Megenagna (መገናኛ)	
21	Kara (ካራ)	
22	Kara - 2 (ካራ)	
23	Sost Kutur Mazoriya (ሶስት ቀጥር ማዞሪያ)	
24	Kaliti (ቃሊቲ)	
25	Gerji (ገርጂ)	
26	Kidane Meheret (ኪዳነ ምህረት)	
27	Alliance Ethio Française (አሊያንስ ኢትዮ ፍራንሴዝ)	
28	Legehar (ለጋር)	
29	Legehar - 2 (ለጋር)	
30	Balderas (ባልደራስ)	
31	Chilot Adebabay (ችሎት አደባባይ)	
32	Salite Meheret (ሰላሊተ ምህረት)	

* Numbers are corresponding to those in Figure 3.

As detailed observations of individual *tera askebari* were needed, tertiary fieldwork was conducted in Megenagna terminal, which is one of the major terminals in Addis Ababa (Figure 4). The fieldwork was conducted from August 24 to October 31, 2019. I used anthropological and ethnographic methods such as participant observation, in-depth interviews, and informal conversations with the *tera askebari* and the minibus workers. Additionally, informal interviews and conversations were conducted with passengers, street vendors, and shoeshines who operate daily, and youth who often stopped by the terminal seeking jobs. I also conducted remote research in Japan through the telephone communication with the informants after the COVID-19 occurrence from February to September 2020.

For comprehensive research, interviews were conducted at government agencies that could provide broader insight into the *tera askebari* to understand the government's perspective. The interviews were conducted with high-ranking officials in the AARTB and the local district offices of the Addis Ababa Job Opportunity Creation and Enterprises Development Bureau (formerly Addis Ababa Micro and Small Enterprise Development Bureau [AAMSEDB]) offices in which the *tera askebari* groups are registered. These interviews provided insights into the government's policies and perspectives regarding the *tera askebari.*

Secondary data regarding transport, unemployment rate, and the Micro and Small Enterprises (MSEs) programs were collected from published resources, such as books, journals, and governmental documents. During the fieldwork, I collected secondary data from academic institutions and several government organizations, such as the Addis Ababa University, Library of Institute of Ethiopian Studies, AARTB, Central Statistical Agency (CSA), and the Addis Ababa Job Opportunity Creation and Enterprises Development Bureau.

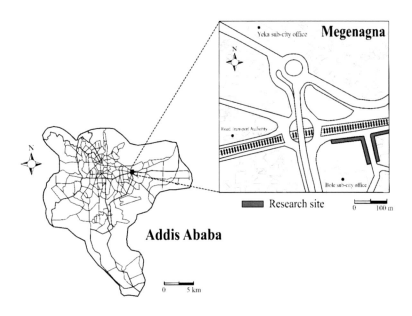

Figure 4. Map of Addis Ababa and research site in the tertiary fieldwork

Scope and limitation

As there was no research on specific classifications of the *tera askebari* groups, the research site for the collection of data was randomly selected. The two fieldwork sessions, which mainly included in-depth interviews with a few participants at various terminals, were effective in determining the characteristics of the various *tera askebari* groups that are present in Addis Ababa. The research was conducted in approximately 30 terminals, which constitute about 20% of the existing terminals in Addis Ababa (AARTB 2019); collecting data from all terminals was not practicable. The results aided in identifying the characteristics of the *tera askebari*'s business, categorizing their business type and in reconstructing the history of the *tera askebari*.

The tertiary fieldwork was conducted in a specific terminal, referred to as Platform X in this thesis. The research was mainly conducted through in-depth interviews with the *tera askebari*, street workers who work at the terminal, passengers, and government officials, as well as participant observation of the *tera askebari*'s behavior. The *tera askebari* at Platform X mostly originated from specific ethnic groups in the southern part of Ethiopia. Most of them speak and operate their business in Amharic, as it is the official language of Ethiopia, but some of the informal discourses among themselves were conducted in their mother tongue, which I was not able to comprehend. However, the majority of their operations were conducted in Amharic, in which I was proficient enough to analyze how they dealt with the minibus workers. Their use of their local language helped me in understanding their origins and the ethnic linkage that existed amongst the *tera askebari* at the terminal.

Organization of the book

This book consists of seven chapters. Chapter 1 represents a general introduction to the thesis, together with the objectives, methodology, and overview of the research site. The major research site was the Megenagna Terminal, which is a major terminal in the eastern part of Addis Ababa.

Chapter 2 presents a literature review related to the study topic. It is largely divided into four parts: debates on the informal economy, transport workers in Africa, public transportation in Addis Ababa, and *tera askebari* in Addis Ababa. First, it has been accentuated to focus on the process of specific cases through which informality is created under the influence of a formal regulatory environment. The major characteristics of the urban transport service in Africa were that the "informalities" were prevailing, where the workers perform their job without regulations and often act transgressively and violently, which has become a norm in the industry. However, it is not their personal characteristics, but it formed through the interactions and influences of the formal environment.

Chapter 3 deals with the historical process of the formation of *tera askebari* in Addis Ababa before the MSEs agency's intervention. *Tera askebari* have developed through the following four processes: (1) street gangs' initiation, (2) designation of Eritrean—Ethiopian war veterans, (3) Gash Abera Molla's social beautification project, and (4) the growth and rise of *tera askebari* under the city's development. The *tera askebari* business was stimulated by street gangs under the turbulent political environment at the end of the 1980s. Weak state governance and the void of adequate transport management spurred the rise of *tera askebari* all over the city, which has developed as an indispensable service in the public transport sector.

Chapter 4 focuses on the dynamics between state and current practice of *tera askebari*, especially focusing on how the *wanna* (boss in the *tera askebari* group) utilize the regulatory environment of MSEs development policy. Under the government's transport policy to sustain current minibus operation and the characteristics of the MSEs program, created a background of *wanna*'s behavioral patterns and enabled them to maintain their power until the current moment.

Chapter 5 discusses the livelihoods and coping strategies of employee *tera askebari* (YBs) who are working at Platform X. Most of the YBs were rural migrants originating from the southern part of Ethiopia, largely from Hadiya, Wolaytta, and Gurage ethnic groups. This special feature was generated through the dragging activities of former YBs, who were mostly living in an immigrant residence called Gurd Shola. Under the insecure employment of informal transport jobs, YBs were seeking and diversifying their working opportunities by continuously visiting the terminal and communicating with other transport workers. The easy accessibility various job opportunities in Platform X worked as a cushion to alleviate a shock from unexpected employment severance.

Chapter 6 aimed to determine the social role of *tera askebari* and their contribution to society by observing their management activities on minibuses and passengers. This chapter largely consisted of three parts: descriptions of *tera askebari*'s activities, their language usage, and passengers' perception of them. *Tera askebari* devised various methods to handle the minibus in the Terminal. Their management showed some degree of flexibility, but certain rules and customs, which were constructed through interactions with minibus operators, inhibited *tera askebari* to abuse their power. Meanwhile, the language that they use mostly consists of the imperative form, which was developed to deliver their message effectively in a crowded and bustling working environment. Lastly, passengers' perception of the *tera askebari* was double sided, in which many people acknowledged their critical roles, while some perceived their activities as insolent and unmethodical.

Chapter 7 presents a summary of the research, findings, and comprehensive discussions and conclusions. This thesis concludes with three points of discussion. First, through YBs' job-seeking activities, transport workers have demonstrated high adaptability and viability for coping with the unstable urban labor market. Second, the *tera askebari* are the main agents shaping public order in the terminals, even with their flexible management style. Third, *tera askebari* are acting a crucial role in maintaining the public order in the terminals, even with their flexible management style. The thesis concludes that the *tera askebari* are *balemuya* (smart strategists) who draw their living strategies by utilizing a in/formality in urban transport.

Notes

[1] *Askebari* is derived from a verb *askebara* (አስከበረ), which means to uphold or enforce the law or property. *Askari* means soldier and a guard in multiple languages such as Swahili, Somali, and Arabic, and it is derived from Persian word of *askari*. The Amharic verb *askebara* is similar with this term, while it is not certain whether this term has a same etymology with the *askari*.

[2] The term *tera askebari* refer to persons who uphold the queue, so there are various kinds of "*tera askebari*" such as those who works at construction site or certain market to keep the customer's sequence.

[3] *Birr* is the Ethiopian currency and 1 *santim* are equivalent to 0.01 *birr*.

[4] Interview from officer at AARTB, August 17, 2019.

Chapter 2. Literature Review

This chapter presents a literature review related to the study topic. It begins with the debates about and development of informal economy analysis. It then explores the literature on transportation workers in Africa. Lastly, it discusses the literature on the public transportation service in Addis Ababa and attempts to find the research gap.

Debates on the informal economy: Static to dynamic analysis

Introduction

Garbage collectors, motorbike taxi drivers, street vendors, and shoeshine boys are informal workers who are easily found in urban Africa. Currently, 60–80% of the jobs and economic activities in urban Africa are provided by the informal sector (International Labour Organization [ILO] 2002: 16; Guven & Karlen 2020). Whereas the formal wage sector is not expected to create sufficient jobs compared to the rapidly growing population, the size and scale of the informal sector are expected to further increase (Guven & Karlen 2020). Under these circumstances, the "informal economy" has become an indispensable concept to explain urban phenomena in modern Africa.

Since the concept was created, the informal economy has been constantly debated in a variety of fields, including economics, politics, development studies, and anthropology. Despite major debates and criticism, the term continues to be widely accepted by various actors such as state authorities, international organizations, and academic researchers (Lindell 2010: 5). To understand how this concept functions on the ground in urban Africa, we need to examine how this concept has been developed since its creation.

Informal vs formal: Early dualism to legalism

The notion of the "informal economy" was first introduced by Hart in the early 1970s (Hart 1973). He focused on small-scale income-generating activities in cities and collectively identified self-employment activities as an "informal sector." As an economic anthropologist, Hart observed the dynamics and possibilities of this sector and believed the informal economy could serve as a safety net for marginalized people in urban areas. Regardless of his intention, the dichotomy of simply dividing economic activity into formal and informal sectors was widely accepted.

In this dualistic perspective, the informal sector was situated as a concept that confronted formality, and it was relegated to the domain of the "pre-modern, traditional, and marginalized," which fails to attain "modern, capitalist, urban, and formal" features (ILO 1972; Bromley 1978: 1034). This perspective observed informal workers negatively, referring to them as deinstitutionalized people who were neglected in the modernized economy and who did not have the willingness to solve the problem. Informal workers in Africa are considered in the same context, as most of their activities have been disregarded as the living strategies of the uneducated, poor, and vulnerable (ILO 2002; Andrews et al. 2011: 6).

The discourse about the informal sector further developed into legalism, which was described by De Soto during the late 1980s (De Soto 1989). In his renowned book, "The Other Path," he questioned the reason behind the poverty in third-world countries under capitalism. He assumed that the reason for poverty was a low registration rate regarding property rights. Because of the high regulatory barrier and demanding bureaucratic procedure, people cannot freely participate in the economic activities of the formal zone. In a condition in which entry into the official sector is difficult, many people have made alternative choices to accumulate wealth through economic activities outside of this regulation (Portes & Schauffler 1993: 40). In other words, the country's inability to meet the basic needs of the majority of the poor led them to take informal measures because they were unable to achieve wealth and economic development. The legalists, including DeSoto, argued that it is essential to fold the informal sector into the formal sector by implementing liberal policies and removing various regulations (De Soto 2001: 42).

Problem of the in/formal dichotomy

Early dualism and legalism divided economic activities and properties into two different areas.[1] However, this approach was not appropriate for understanding the complex features of the human economy. First, this strategy did not effectively capture the complex and mixed cases that occurred between those sections. Based on De Soto's argument, paratransit services are "informal" if the operators lack a legal license. However, there are various forms of contracts and links between the operators, who operate privately or work with a legal license that can be situated between the formal and informal sectors (Rasmussen 2012; Pirie 2013: 13). These types of complexities cannot be fully explained by the dualistic and legalistic views, which confine the informal sector to isolated areas with specific characteristics.

The other problem was that the formal—informal dichotomy impedes observation of the informal economy with an unbiased view. The formal economy was regarded as comparatively superior, and the informal economy was considered unmodernized, unsystematic, and deficient to the formal (ILO 2002; Trebilcock 2005: 21). The dichotomy has also subordinated other parts of the informal economy in a negative manner, such as considering the informal employment as exploitative, deleterious, and low-security and the workers as having no will or abilities (Williams et al. 2007: 404). However, informal activities often occur in highly institutionalized economies as well as developed countries (Castells & Portes 1989: 13; Carré 2017; Kim & Milner 2019: 520). This illustrates that the dichotomy may not be efficient for understanding the various phenomena occurring in the current world.

Focus on the process of shaping the informality

Since the 1980s, scholars have attempted to understand the relationship between the formal and informal economies. According to the structuralist approach, the informal economy is effectively conceptualized by something that is "not" (Castells & Portes 1989: 12). Castells and Portes highlighted the state regulations as key variables and understood the informal economy as income-generating activities that operate outside the state regulatory boundaries (Castells & Portes 1989). Unlike the former views that attempt to attribute specific characteristics to the informal sector, structuralists view the informal economy as flexible.[2] According to this approach, informal activities are influenced and formulated through their interactions with the formal sector, and they also contain some degree of formality. Therefore, instead of the term "informal sector," which delimits its boundary of concept, "informality," which can express the interrelationships between various economic forms and spaces, started to be used for the theoretical and practical implications (Chae 2015: 107-108).

Currently, scholars are trying to focus their attention on specific cases, a process through which informality is created under the influence of a formal regulatory environment. Lindell said, "Informality needs to be situated in specific contexts, as there is great geographical variation in the forms that economic informality takes and in the ways in which they relate to state regulation" (2010: 5). As she noted, the informal economy is heterogeneous, displaying different characteristics in accordance with geographical areas.[3] Thus, understanding "informality" should not simply be treated as the territory outside formal regulation; however, investigating social backgrounds, actors' strategies, and processes of government intervention should be considered to fully understand the dynamics of informality.

This approach unfolded the domain of informal economy research in various fields, particularly those associated with informal workers' livelihood activities and strategies. Often, informal workers are viewed as vulnerable individuals (Tokman 2007; Makoma 2018), but their ability to cope with various problems and overcome hardships has received more attention (Moser 1998; Bauman 2004). Their ability to create networks inside and outside rural and urban settings has also attracted attention (Mary 2010; Hansen 2015; Phanuel 2016). The capacity of informal workers to collectively act and raise political voices has received extensive recognition (Bayat 2004; Villancourt-Laflamme 2005; Britwum & Akorsu 2017; Rizzo & Atzeni 2020) despite their lack of organizational capacity (Meagher 2010). Their activities were also acknowledged in the public sector for providing various public services that the government failed to provide (Harper 2000; Andreasen & Møller-Jensen 2016). As suggested in the aforementioned studies, we can broaden our thinking to understand the elusive features of "informality" when we deviate our views from the classical dichotomy and focus on people's activities on the ground level.

Transport workers in Africa

Paratransit in Africa

Car Rapide in Senegal, *Matatu* in Kenya, *Tro-tro* in Ghana, and the minibus in Addis Ababa are "paratransit" services operating in Africa, and such services typically describe minibus services that operate without a fixed schedule. Since the 1980s, the use of paratransit services has increased in response to the void of government services in many African cities. Currently, its importance of paratransit services has unprecedentedly increased, making it difficult to operate cities without these services (Kumar & Barrett 2008: 6; UN Habitat 2013: 26-27; Klopp & Cavoli 2018). They play a major role in running urban mobility; for example, *Kombis* in Harare accounts for 90% of the total mobility in the transportation sector, versus 73% for the minibus in Durban and 70% for *Matatu* in Nairobi (Howe & Bryceson 2000: 37; Venter et al. 2007: 662; Pirie 2013: 13; AARTB 2012). These services helped many citizens to move and access various facilities and participate in educational, health, and recreational activities (Palmer

& Berrisford 2015: 13). In particular, this sector has contributed to reducing the inequality of urban services by providing transportation services in underdeveloped areas inaccessible by public transportation (Lucas 2011). It also created various work opportunities for youths, such as driving and touting and allied jobs such as mechanics, marshals, shoe shiners, and street venders at the terminal (Pirie 2014: 135). Because of its easy entry and a lack of a requirement for extensive skills, many youths who migrated from rural areas or those who have not benefited from educational services could participate in economic activities (Tilahun 2014: 124).

Meanwhile, paratransit has often been criticized because it causes traffic and environmental problems. With urbanization, the number of vehicles has increased rapidly to meet the transportation demand. Paratransit has caused heavy traffic congestion because the vehicles are smaller than those used for public transportation, which occupies a large space on the road (Pirie 2013: 15-16). In addition, paratransit services cause high levels of greenhouse gas emissions, as most of the vehicles are outdated cars (Pirie 2013: 32; Amegah & Agyei-Mensah 2017: 741).

Transport workers in Africa

Despite the benefits and drawbacks, the paratransit sector has been a point at which various cultural, social, political, and artistic areas intersect beyond the dimension of mobility. First, paratransit has been a critical issue in politics. In particular, transportation operators have participated in notable collective movements such as demonstrations and strikes in response to the government's enforcement in Addis Ababa and Nairobi (Abbink 2006: 186; Kenda 2006: 555-556). In this regard, transportation workers were often portrayed as strong entities who could rally political voices against the government. They also have an influence on the public, as they can mobilize the public to participate in collective movements, which often forced the government to implement certain regulations (Kenda 2017: 159; Davison 2019: 71). Therefore, many African governments have attempted to sway transportation workers to achieve their political goals (Di Nunzio 2014: 452; Davison 2019: 70-71).

In the cultural dimension, mutual support networks are often observed among the drivers. For example, in Ghana, the lorry drivers have a saving system to help elderly drivers who are no longer able to work (Hart 2016: 145). Transportation is also a medium that often creates a new culture. For instance, the *Matatu* sub-culture of young men has developed unique manners and styles of speech and vocabulary (James 2018). Their language has also received attention, being captured in people's narratives regarding transportation workers and the phrases and expressions used in the vehicles (Mbugua & Samper 2006; Onchiri 2010). Additionally, it is well known that transportation vehicles are canvases for young artists to express their ideas and ideologies with their unique styles throughout West and East Africa (Glader 2017; Africa News and Reuters 2018; Holloway 2019; Kamau 2020)

In the anthropological field, many studies have observed the activities of hired workers, especially their touting activities and livelihoods. These studies largely focused on the insecure environment of transportation workers, as their contracts do not have legal protection and their incomes are low (Richard & Happy 2008: 219; Rizzo 2011: 1185; AfDB 2013; Doherty 2017; Siyabulela 2021). Because of these reasons, African transportation workers were largely portrayed as vulnerable individuals who are easily affected by the capitalistic system and state policies.

Meanwhile, several studies examined transportation workers' coping strategies. In Ghana, long-distance drivers have mutual support networks that provide assistance in times of crisis (Hart 2016: 144-145). In addition, these workers have forged close relationships with market women and other traders to ensure that they have sufficient food for their travels (Hart 2016: 145). Also, transportation workers use various strategies in times when work is not possible. For example, the call boys in Malawi adopt strategies such as street vending and charcoal making when they face state bans on touting practices (Richard & Happy 2008).

Paratransit and the informalities

As previously explained, paratransit plays a crucial role in citizens' movement and their access to various facilities across Africa. Because of the insufficient governance capacity and lack of proper institutional setup, the paratransit sector has been growing, resulting in overloading, speeding, charging additional costs, and traffic jams. These so-called "informalities" and rules transgressions have been "norms" in this industry (Agbiboa 2020). Meanwhile, transportation workers earn a few cents each day, which has caused them to become more volatile and transgressive (Rizzo 2011). Thus, these "informalities" of paratransit are not intrinsic characteristics, but they should be understood as part of people's daily survival within the larger context of politics and the global system. For example, in Lagos, Nigeria, informal motor-park touts emerged under the unstable social condition of the structural adjustment program during the 1980s (Agbiboa 2018). In Kenya, the government's indifference to developing public transportation services has influenced the growth of *Matatu* businesses through illegal political movement (Rasmussen 2012). In this regard, it is significant to observe what is happening on the ground and understand how the concept of "informalities" influence and utilized by the transport workers in Africa to identify further possibilities of African urban transportation.

Despite diverse studies applying the concept of informalities in the transport sector in Africa, the transportation workers' strategies after the formalization of their business have not received academic attention. First, most paratransit businesses in Africa still operate privately. Second, "formalization" in many African countries was meant to alter paratransit services into a modern public bus system, which is often called the Bus Rapid Transit service. *Tera askebari* in Addis Ababa is a distinctive and unique case in Africa in which the informal transportation business has been formalized as a legal private enterprise. To date, the studies on African transportation have focused on the activities, livelihoods, and survival strategies of daily workers. However, this approach was not successful in clarifying the full meaning of "informalities." My research focuses on the daily activities of *tera askebari* for both legal and illegal statuses. I observe how both statuses of *tera askebari* cross the boundary of formal and informal and layout their strategies. This has not been researched previously, and my research can provide a new angle for understanding the "informalities" of paratransit in Africa in a comprehensive manner.

Public transportation in Addis Ababa

Development of the public transportation service in Addis Ababa

Public transport service before the minibus

Modern public transportation in Ethiopia began during the Fascist Italian occupation (1936–1941). Fascist Italy invaded Ethiopia in 1935, and its rule from 1936 to 1941 influenced the early stage of transportation development in the country.[4] The initial public transportation service began with intercity buses that connected Addis Ababa to other major cities. Two routes, namely from Addis Ababa to Dire Dawa and Asmara, were operated initially by the Italian company Compagnia Italiana Transporti Africa Orientale (Pankhurst 1968; Habtai 1987). Subsequently, services between major cities were provided. The Italian government launched a project to build approximately 10,000 km of roads in Ethiopia. They completed 6,000 km of this goal, and this infrastructure later catalyzed the intercity transportation service between the major cities (Talbot 1952: 140-144; Podestà 2013).

Although Italy's road development policy led to the growth of intercity buses, there was no significant development concerning public transportation in Addis Ababa. The public transportation system in Addis Ababa was affected by the Italian segregation policy. In that era, Ethiopians were restricted from using certain facilities and services used by Italians (see Elias 2018: 38-39; Imam & Yonas 2018: 128). These measures were also applied during the early stages of transportation planning, during which politicians attempted to block the usage of transportation vehicles by Ethiopians (Mariani 1938; Pankhurst 1973: 112). For example, the taxicab business was actively operated by an Italian taxicab company, but Ethiopians were restricted from using it. Because of restrictions on the use of transportation services for the local population and Italy's prioritization of its own citizens for these services, the public transportation service did not actively develop during the early 1930s.

Public transportation services began to develop after Emperor Haile Selassie regained power in 1941. The first public transportation service was developed in 1940–1942 by using vehicles abandoned by Italians, which led to the development of private—public transportation services (Eshetie et al. 2013: 723). After the invasion ended, many vehicles that were owned by Italians were confiscated and sold to Ethiopians and foreigners, thereby creating a conducive environment for participation in the transportation business (FTA 2020). The initial service was provided by 150 Volkswagen Kombi vehicles (Table 3). The Kombi accommodated approximately 10 people with a Bongo vehicle and provided services similar to the current minibuses, which can pick up passengers during the route (Pankhurst 1958; Burgoyne 1967). The other type was a public bus, termed an *anbessa* bus (አንበሳ አውቶቡስ, literally means "lion bus"). The *anbessa* bus started service with 10 vehicles in 1952, and the number of routes has increased with the city's growth (see Eshetie et al. 2013: 723). During this era, the Ethiopian government made various efforts to develop public transportation. During the Third Five Year Plan (1968–1972), the government devoted 7.7 million Ethiopian *birr*[5] to the development of public bus services and 4.6 million *birr* to private transportation systems. [6]

Table 3. Types of public transportation in Addis Ababa in the 1950s

Type of service	Type of conveyance	Type of fuel	Fleets
Intercity	Omnibus	Diesel	200
	Bus (Volkswagen)	Petrol	300
Intercity and inner city	*Anbessa* bus	Petrol	-
	Microbuses (Volkswagen Kombi)	Petrol	150
	Taxi (Fiat Seicentos)	Petrol	280

Note: Adopted from Pankhurst (1958).

Minibus service in the Derg regime (1974–1991)

The minibus service was initiated during the *Derg* socialist regime (ደርግ). During this time, the Road Transport Authority office (የመንገድ ትራንስፖርት ባለሥልጣን መስሪያ ቤት) replaced the Road Transport Administration (የመንገድ ትራንስፖርት አስተዳደር) operated by the imperial government. During this time, Proclamation No. 107/69 was issued to improve transportation management, including changes to speed limits, tariff rules, and loadings.

During the 1980s, a bulk of used Toyota Hi-Ace minibuses was imported into the city. Vehicles that operated under the taxi services were painted blue and white to distinguish them from normal vehicles. During this time, the government established corporations and a zoning system called *kat'ena* (ቀጠና), and the minibus workers worked on designated lines under this system (FTA 2020). In addition, it was mentioned that the payment tariff for minibuses should follow government regulations. In general, the road transportation service was fully regulated by the *Derg* government in the early time. However, after approximately 10 years of operation, the minibus service was privatized, and minibuses could freely operate their business.[7]

Minibus service in the Ethiopian People's Revolutionary Democratic Front (EPRDF) era (1991–)

After the liberal government led by EPRDF gained power in 1991, the public transportation service entered a new phase. During this time, commercial public transportation services including minibuses could operate independently without state control, and any qualified person was allowed to enter the commercial transportation business. Meanwhile, the previous zoning system was abolished, and minibuses were allowed to operate in any terminal.

In 2012, the Addis Ababa city administration established the AARTB to better control the city's public transportation. Subsequently, AARTB has become the major institution overseeing public transportation issues in the city, as it can announce and enforce the regulations regarding the paratransit business in the city.

Types of public transportation in Addis Ababa

With the development of public transportation services, multiple types of public transportation have emerged in Addis Ababa. The first type is scheduled public transportation, which functions according to a fixed schedule. Concerning road transportation, *anbessa* and *sheger* buses (ሸገር አውቶቡስ) are operated by the municipal enterprises Anbessa City Bus Service Enterprise and AARTB (Figure 5). *Anbessa* buses have been operating since the 1960s, and *Sheger* buses were introduced in 2017 to meet the growing traffic demand. From 2009 to 2018, the commercial public bus services *Alliance* (አሊያንስ አውቶቡስ)[8] and *Axion* (አክሲዮን አውቶቡስ) were operational, but these services were suspended because of persistent deficits. Regarding railway transportation, the Light Railway service, which is operated jointly by the Ethiopia Railway Corporation and Chinese Shenzhen Metro Group, operates across the city with two major lines.

Figure 5. *Anbessa* bus at Arat Kilo area (October 18, 2019)

The other type of public transportation is commercial transportation, which is operated by private (often called informal) operators. The first type is the minibus service (Figure 6). It is the most commonly used transportation service, being used by 90% of daily transportation users (AARTB 2012). Whereas minibuses operate on most of the routes in Addis Ababa, mid-sized buses, named *Higer* (ሀይገር)[9] and *Lonchon* (ሎንቾን), operate on some specific routes to support minibuses in areas with large numbers of users (Figures 7 and 8, respectively). These buses usually accept 25–40 passengers. Due to their appearance, mid-sized buses received special nicknames. *Higer* is often called *k'ando* (ቀንዶ, horns)[10] as it has two big side mirrors that are similar to the horns of an animal. *Lonchon* is often called *k'et'e k'et'e* (ቅጥቅጥ) to reflect the creaky sound it makes because of its old vehicle parts. Another type of commercial transportation is the four-wheel taxicab service. For a long time, this service has been dominated by taxi operators called *lada* (ላዳ) (Figure 9), but currently, meter taxis have been introduced, including Ze-lucy, Comfort, and the ride-hailing services Ride and Feres (Figures 10 and 11). In addition, tricycle service for short-distance transportation called *bajaji* (ባጃጅ, tricycle transport) is available in some parts of the city in which the minibus service is not provided (Figure 12).

Figure 6. Minibus at the Faransai roundabout (July 19, 2018)

Figure 7. *Higer* **bus at the Megenagna Terminal, Kazanchis direction (August 23, 2019)**

Figure 8. *K'et'e k'et'e* **at Sebeta, Oromia region (October 29, 2016)**

Figure 9. *Lada* **taxi at the Megenagna Terminal (September 17, 2019)**

Figure 10. Meter taxi, Ze-Lucy at Mabrat Hail Condominium (July 27, 2017)

Figure 11. Meter taxi, Comfort at Signal Condominium (August 5, 2019)

Figure 12. *Bajaj* gathered in the center of Gurd Shola (September 9, 2019)

Characteristics of the minibus business in Addis Ababa

Among various types of transportation, the minibus is undoubtedly playing the leading role because of its easy accessibilities and ability to provide rapid service compared to formal transportation vehicles, which depart at designated times and accommodate a large number of passengers. For example, the average waiting time of passengers for minibuses is 12 minutes, versus 86 minutes for the *anbessa* bus (AATA 2017). In addition, the number of vehicles is incomparable relative to the other types of transportation. Although 18,681 minibuses are registered to the city transport bureau, the numbers of *anbessa*, *higer*, and *lonchon* buses are total 600, 166, and 92, respectively (AARTB 2019). For this reason, the minibus has emerged as a major transportation vehicle in the city, serving approximately 90% of the citizen's mobility needs.

The minibus business is a commercial business in which each vehicle operates privately. Most drivers are contract operators who borrow vehicles from the owners and pay usage fees. Sometimes, owners drive their own cars instead of lending them to other drivers. The daily rental payment is 400–600 *birr* depending on the condition of the vehicle, and this amount accounts for more than half of operators' net earnings. Whereas the owner is responsible for paying the insurance fee and association fee, it is the driver's responsibility to pay the license extension fee, purchase gas, and repair the vehicle's components as needed, which account for most of the maintenance costs. This situation has caused workers to struggle for higher profits, leading them to work aggressively, drive at high speeds, and collect extra charges from the passengers.

The attendants are subcontracted by the drivers, and most of them are rural migrant workers who moved to the city for a better life. These workers are called *redat* (ረዳት), which means a supporter or assistant of the driver, but they are often called *weyala* (ወያላ) in insolent ways. Another nickname for these workers is *DJ-wu* (ዲጄው), as they are considered the DJ in the car. Their contracts are mostly verbal agreements that lack social security. Their daily wage is 100–400 *birr*, or approximately 4–14 USD, and the amount varies depending on the contract they made. However, in some cases, *redat* are relatives of the vehicle owner or people who made a secret contract with the owners to surveil whether the driver damaged the car or cheated on the income. These workers are called *enba* (እንባ, tear) because they often discomfort the drivers. The attendant's major role is to tout passengers, charge the fares, and notify drivers to stop and start the vehicles during a passenger's stopover and boarding by tapping the vehicles door and saying "*sab*," meaning "to depart" (the vehicles).

The minibus fare is determined according to the length of the trip. In 2019, the tariff rate was 1.5 *birr* for a 2.5km trip (see Table 4). Based on this criterion, the minibus fare ranged from 1.5 to 12 *birr*. As an example, the length of the Semit Terminal is 7.5 km, which is applied to the 5.1–7.5 section. Thus, the fare of this route is 4.5 *birr*. The minibus fare has been increasing since 2012, and as of September 2020, the fare has increased to 2 *birr* per 2.5 km. In 2021, the minibus tariff increased again to 2.5 *birr* per 2.5 km because of the recent increase in oil prices (2Markato 2022).

Because of their high expenses, many minibus drivers often try to make money fast, resulting in transgressive behavior. They often overload passengers, drive at excessive speeds (Fekadu 2014: 125), charge additional costs to passengers (Tilahun 2014: 125), and tout irregularly (Fekadu 2013: 69).[11] To tackle such issues, two government institutions and *tera askebari* are working to regulate the minibuses in different aspects. First, the traffic police are concerned about the overloading of minibuses. Depending on the vehicle type and performance, the number of passengers that minibuses can accept ranges from 12 to 15. Old minibuses, which usually have a code-1 license plate, are required to

Table 4. Minibus tariff by distance from 2012 to 2021

Distance (km)			Year					
			2012	2017	2018	Sep 07, 2020	2021	Dec 17, 2021
			Fare (*birr*)					
0.0	-	2.5	1.35	1.45	1.50	2.00	2.00	2.50
2.6	-	5.0	2.70	2.70	3.00	4.00	4.50	5.00
5.1	-	7.5	3.75	3.95	4.50	6.00	6.50	7.50
7.6	-	10.0	3.90	5.20	6.00	8.00	9.00	10.00
10.1	-	12.5	5.00	6.45	7.50	10.00	11.00	12.50
12.6	-	15.0			9.00	12.00	13.00	15.00
15.1	-	17.5			10.5	14.00	15.50	17.50
17.6	-	20.0			12.0	16.00	17.50	20.00
20.1	-	22.5					20.00	22.50
22.6	-	25.0					22.00	25.00
25.1	-	27.5					24.00	27.50

Source: Author's own observation and reference to AARTB (2012) and 2Merkato (2022).

accept 12 passengers (Figure 13).[12] This is because most of these vehicles have been used for more than 30 years. Code-3 licensed vehicles, such as Toyota Hi-Ace 5-L or 3-L (locally called *Abadula* and Dolphin), are comparatively new vehicles with the *gulbet* (ጉልበት, power) to accept more passengers (Figure 14).[13] They can accept 15 people in vehicles with three seats per row. For the safety of the passengers, the traffic police take legal measures when minibuses overload passengers beyond the seat limit.

The other institution is AARTB, which investigates the volume of traffic and transportation needs in each terminal through individual agents called *tek'ot'et'ari* (ተቆጣጣሪ, auditor) and decides the work routes for each minibus (Figures 15 and 16). Subsequently, the AARTB gives a *tapella* (ታፔላ, route indicator) to the driver that indicates the operating route of the minibus. The *tapella* can be installed on top of the vehicle using an iron board (Figure 17), but sometimes, AARTB issues a permission letter for their operation, which is called *wust' tapella* (ውስጥ ታፔላ, route indicator inside the vehicle) or *werek'et tapella* (ወረቀት ታፔላ, route indicator made with paper; Figure 18). Nevertheless, because of the lucrativeness of the routes, existence of passengers, and favorable working conditions, minibus workers often work on undesignated routes. Thus, the prime objective of AARTB in minibus management is to monitor the operation of minibuses on designated routes, and drivers who violate the regulation face legal measures, such as penalty points and fines (see Figure 19). If drivers work without a *tapella*, they are fined 500 *birr*, and if they drive on an undesignated route, they are fined 200 *birr*. When considering that their daily net earnings are 400–600 *birr*, these fines represent considerable penalties.

The last agencies concerned with minibus management are the *tera askebari* groups. *Tera askebari* groups are private enterprises that are registered in the city's MSEs development program. Unlike the aforementioned institutions, the management activities of *tera askebari* are private. They do not receive any traffic information from AARTB or guidance and training in managing the minibuses. With 138 *tera askebari* groups spread all over the city,[14] they operate independently and control minibuses according to their own standards.

Figure 13. Code-1 minibus (Bole Arabsa Condominium, October 3, 2019)

Figure 14. Code-3 minibus (National Theatre, September 2, 2019)

Figure 15. *Tek'ot'et'ari* **sitting at the parasol during break time (Piazza Arada Terminal, July 15, 2018)**

Figure 16. Two *tek'ot'et'ari* **(fluorescence jacket and one in the middle) talking with the driver (right) (Ayat Terminal, September 2, 2019)**

Figure 17. License plate (top) and iron *tapella* (below) (taken at the AARTB office, September 2, 2019)

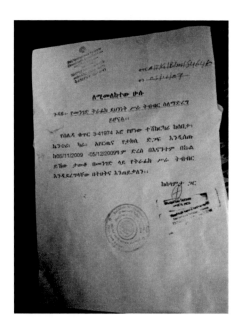

Figure 18. Operating permission from AARTB, which is called *wust' tapella* or *werek'et tapella* (July 13, 2017)

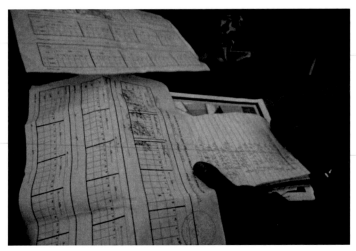

Figure 19. *Tek'ot'et'ari* **checking the attendance of minibuses and signing the attendance sheet (Megenagna Terminal, September 3, 2019)**

Summary

Since its origin in the 1970s, the term "informal economy" has been constantly debated. Early analysis regarded the informal sector as existing separately from the formal sector, and it is described as traditional, modern, and underdeveloped. However, this dichotomy was not sufficient for understanding complex features of the economy such as employment, salary, and personal motivation. Since the 1980s, the "informal economy" started to be understood as economic activities that operate outside the state regulatory boundaries. This categorization was sufficient for understanding how the informal economy was created, as any phenomenon can be formal or informal based on the regulation. In this regard, the term "informality," which can express the degree of formal and informal and reflect the interrelationship between various economic forms and spaces, started to be used for the theoretical and practical implications. Because "informality" is heterogeneous and it cannot be determined as one specific characteristic, it is required to investigate the social background, actors' strategies, and processes of government intervention to understand its dynamics.

In Africa, paratransit plays a major role in serving urban transportation needs. This service provides an essential service by providing access to various modern facilities in cities and works as an employment pool by creating various working opportunities. The paratransit sector has been a point at which various cultural, social, political, and artistic areas intersect and mix beyond the dimension of mobility. In the anthropological field, transportation workers were often considered weak and vulnerable because of their low job security and economic status. Meanwhile, the strategies transportation workers use to manage crises were also discussed.

Why do "informalities" in the paratransit sector matter? Paratransit in Africa can be critical for understanding the concept of informalities. In Africa, many operators, drivers, and owners frequently cross the boundaries of formal and informal to ensure their survival or increase their profits. For this reason, notorious social practices such as overloading, overcharging, cheating, and speeding are still ongoing. The transgression of rules has become an ordinary phenomenon in African industries. Thus, we should understand these practices in line with people's daily survival in the larger context of politics and the global system. *Tera askebari* in Addis Ababa is a distinctive and unique case in Africa in which the informal transportation business has been formalized as a legal private enterprise, but informal practices have remained operational. By observing *tera askebari*'s practices, which have not been researched previously, we can understand how formal and informal activities are interconnected and how urban youths are cleverly utilizing the concept of informality to survive in the ever-changing urban landscape of Addis Ababa.

Notes

[1] De Soto's analysis was based on a three-way split of activity and property: legal, extra-legal, and illegal; synonymous with formal, informal, and criminal. The key to this approach is a separation of means and ends. If means and ends are legal, the activity or property is legal. If ends are legal but means are blocked by unnecessary bureaucratic procedures, unjust charges, prohibited by an unjust law, or arbitrary administrative decision, the activity or property is extra-legal. If both means and ends are illegal, the activity or property is illegal (also, see Bromley 2004: 273).

[2] This idea is grounded in the structuralist principle that views the object as determined by its relationship with other objects, and not by the properties and functions of the object itself (see Portes & Haller 2010: 404-405 as well).

[3] It is also pointed out by Al Sayyad (2004: 27).

[4] During this period, Proclamation No. 11/1934 on road transport has been issued which states the obligation of municipalities to register the motor vehicles (FTA 2020).

[5] 1 USD = 2.481 ETB (Treasury Reporting Rates of Exchange as of March 31, 1968). Treasury Department Fiscal Service Bureau of Accounts.

[6] This plan aims for the social and economic development of the country, aiming to achieve 6% of economic growth and achieve 150USD GDP per capita.

[7] Interview of Mr. Dengelu conducted by informant. Former minibus driver. 72 years old. at *At'ena tera* (Oct 22, 2020).

[8] *Alliance* bus started its operation in 2009 with 50 buses imported from China. In 2016, they imported 100 buses through loan obtained from Commercial Bank of Ethiopia. However, their operation could not persist as they were not able to make enough profits and were not able to repay the loans (See Ethiopian Business Review 2018).

[9] *Higer* received its name from the company's name, Higer Bus.

[10] *K'ando*'s original word is *k'and* (ቀንድ), which means horn. The suffix -o is used as definite article to redound to noun's characteristic.

[11] Also, see Daniel Agbiboa (2020).

[12] These vehicles are registered in the Addis Ababa city. The code-1 license plate is only given to the vehicles that registered to do the transport business. Moreover, most of the vehicles are affiliated to the Automobile Owners Association (የታክሲ ባለንጀሮች ማህበር).

[13] The code-3 minibuses are regarded as commercial vehicles. Most of these vehicles are registered in the Oromia region, a regional state that surrounds Addis Ababa, so the "OR" is written on their license plate as well. Since the minibuses with code-1 license could not meet the growing number of passengers, the city government accepted the private minibuses that used to work on intercity lines, to operate in Addis Ababa around 2017.

[14] Based on the interview and research on 2019.

Chapter 3. History of the Formation and Growth of *Tera Askebari*

This chapter presents the history of the *tera askebari* from the time of their formation up to the current moment. The chapter aims to reconstruct the history of the *tera askebari* and understand how a street gang's business could expand throughout the city and become an essential public service in Addis Ababa. There are three related research questions. First, how was the *tera askebari* business formed? Second, what is the operational mechanism of the *tera askebari* business? Third, how did the *tera askebari* business spread across the city and develop into a fundamental service in the public transport system in Addis Ababa? This chapter is divided into three parts: the initial formation process of the *tera askebari*, mainly by street gangster groups; the creation of the *tera askebari* led by two social projects; and the significance and implications of the citywide expansion of the *tera askebari*.

Street youths' initiative of the *tera askebari* business

The beginning of the tera askebari in the late 1980s

The work of the *tera askebari* originated among urban street youths in the Piazza area in the late 1980s, when the power of the *Derg* regime was waning. The *Derg*, or "committee" or "council" in Amharic, was a military junta that overthrew the Ethiopian Empire in 1974. After seizing power, *Derg* and post-*Derg* governments ruled the country until 1991.[1] By the late 1980s, the country was ravaged by civil war, economic decline, drought, and famine, which affected millions of people. Due to the unstable situation, the *Derg* government, occupied in resolving the unstable domestic situation, could not pay much attention to local affairs.

The minibus service, beginning in the 1980s during the *Derg* period,[2] offered a faster service than the municipal transport, known as the *anbessa* bus. Its weak operational performance and long time-intervals ensured that most citizens did not favor the *anbessa* bus (Eshetie et al. 2013: 726-727; Berhanu 2017). The minibus, preferred by most citizens, quickly became the city's most popular means of public transportation (Macrae 2010: 5). The minibus service was run by the *Derg* government for the first 10 years, whereafter the business was privatized, a development leading to its rise and expansion (Tilahun 2014).[3] The absence of traffic regulations and the government's indifference to the sector and preoccupation with internal affairs allowed street youths to thrive and strengthen their power in the street, seizing the opportunity to start various illegal business activities in the center of Addis Ababa (Di Nunzio 2014: 448).

Among the many attempts to define the concept of "gang," I would like to follow Miller's description, which determines the most common elements of gangs. According to Miller, a youth gang is a "self-formed association of peers, bound together by mutual interests, with identifiable leadership, well-developed lines of authority, and other organizational features, who act in concert to achieve a specific purpose which generally includes the conduct of illegal activity and control over a particular territory, facility, or type of enterprise" (1980: 136). In other words, youth gangs have a well-organized characteristic of mutual cooperation within a structured form of network and commit delinquent acts or conduct illegal activities in a specific area. Without having official ownership, the street gang believe that they are valid rulers entitled to rule the specific territory (see Glaser 2000: 8-9; Shaw 2002: 7; Heinonen 2011: 126-127). This gives street groups legitimacy to access and of local facilities and multiple resources, with the right to recruit members and demand street tax from the street vendors (La Fontaine 1970). In Addis Ababa, the minibus terminal was one of the lucrative resources for the street groups and they launched the *tera askebari* business by taking advantage of the government's low involvement in the minibus business.

The initial *tera askebari* business was started in the late 1980s in the center of the city, in Piazza, by two street gang leaders. "The work started during the time of Mengistu Haile Mariam.[4] Two leaders of the Piazza Arada group commenced this line of work. At the time, there were not many terminals because the city was not as big as it is now" (Mr. Kassahun. 50s. *Tera askebari*. July 10, 2018, Piazza Arada). Mr. Kassahun related the story of the early *tera askebari* while sitting under a parasol collecting money from his subordinate workers. He spoke of two bosses of the Piazza group powerful enough to hire the workers and collect money from the drivers with ease. While it is not clear whether the two leaders created the *tera askebari* business, it seems likely that it was initiated by the street groups.

Rules of collection: Gulbetegna (strong men) claiming tolls from minibus workers

Historically, it was common in Africa for gangs or street boys to be involved in the taxi business. In some cases, taxi operators contracted with street gangs to protect their assets (Bank 1991: 131-132). In most cases, the gang initiated and was involved in operating the minibus business (Kenda 2006: 558-559; Agbiboa 2018: 68). Violence and intimidation were their primary techniques of operation: they used their higher physical and social status in the street economy to maintain their power (Shaw 2002: 74; Isaac 2013: 108; Gibbs 2014: 433). Street groups that initiated the *tera askebari* used the same methods; most of them were members of street groups—referred to as *gulbetegna*[5]—and had superior physical strength. They had control of a certain territory, called *sefer* (ሰፈር, neighborhood), in which they exercised power and collected tolls from minibus workers for "using their area." The two narratives below show how the early gangsters utilized their power to run the *tera askebari*.

Mr. Getahun said:

> *"I started this work under the power of my brother. We moved from Jimma to Addis Ababa when I was 18. My brother was a powerful duriye (ዱሪዬ, vagrant or street boy who behaves badly) in Bole Terminal, so it was easy for me to start working as a tera askebari. It was a better means of earning money than other types of work"* (Mr. Getahun. 20s. Tera askebari. July 7, 2017, Bole Bras Terminal).

Mr. Elias said:

> *"When we first started this job, it was during the Mengistu Haile Mariam period. At that time, the government did not intervene in our affairs. Because Bizuneh's brother was a gangster leader, we worked under his leadership. One day, he passed away, so Bizuneh and I inherited the work. The other group was at Arat Kilo, and we did not touch each other"* (Mr. Elias. 40s. Tera askebari. July 12, 2018, Megenagna Terminal).

Mr. Getahun and Mr. Elias told me how they were affiliated with the work. First, Mr. Getahun explained that he could easily start the *tera askebari* work because of his brother's power. His brother was a powerful *duriye*, which refers to a youngster with vulgar behavior who makes their livelihood on the street. In his narratives, the term *duriye* contains the power and influence that his brother had in his *sefer*. Like Mr. Getahun, Mr. Elias said he was able to start the business because he was a member of the street community. The street group that he belonged to was well-organized and was influential in the Megenagna area, and this enabled Mr. Elias' group to continue the *tera askebari* business.

Meanwhile, it appears that quarrels occasionally occurred between minibus operators and *tera askebari* regarding the services. "There were many fights because some *weyala* (ወያላ, insolent way to refer to minibus assistants) often refused to pay" (Mr. Getahun. 20s. *Tera askebari*. July 05, 2017, Bole Bras Terminal). Mr. Getahun's response demonstrates the apparent tension between the *tera askebari* and minibus operators in the early stages. Minibus operators could work comparatively easily because the *tera askebari* gave orders, but they may have resented the *tera askebari*'s conduct and service charges. However, the *tera askebari*'s dominance and influence in the specific area, together with their belligerent behavior, maintained their power and their business. They used abusive measures—such as chasing minibuses away, threatening drivers, or refusing to allow intractable minibus drivers to work at their terminal—which coerced the operators into abiding by their rules. The *tera askebari*'s influence in their territory forced the minibuses to pay tolls: "There would be a problem if we did not pay the fee. We might not be able to work here anymore" (minibus driver. 40s. September 6, 2019).

The *tera askebari*'s domination in the early days can also be understood in the Ethiopian context. Historically, Ethiopia had a feudal system, in which lords collects tribute from households, enabling their maintenance of power. The pattern of social interaction in Ethiopia has been sustained as strictly hierarchical, in that one person is constrained to obey the "orders from above" (Vaughan & Tronvoll 2003: 32). The traditional feudal system ended after 1974, Addis Ababa experienced rapid urbanization, and the traditional notion of power and authority was transformed and transferred to principally masculine, strong figures who exerted power in the streets.

Power struggle between street groups to take over the tera askebari business

In the 1990s, the *tera askebari* business was run by street groups based on four regions —Piazza, Arat Kilo, Sidist Kilo, and Markato—which was the center of the city at that time.[6] The *tera askebari* business, which was a relatively easy way for street gangsters to make money, led to power struggles in the 1990s among some groups who wanted to take over the terminals of other groups.

Street groups often went on expeditions to conquer another group's territory or made preemptive attacks to defend their territory (Figure 20). According to Di Nunzio's literature (2019: 68-69), a *YeAmerica Gibbi* (የአሜሪካ ግቢ, translated literally as gate of America) group in the Markato region attempted to take over Piazza in the 1990s with the aim of taking over the *tera askebari* business. On hearing this news, Piazza's leader called in his neighbors and fighters, as well as his *tera askebari* members, to carry out a raid on *YeAmerica Gibbi*. In this battle, the Piazza group won the fight, defended their business, and consolidated their governance and influence over the Piazza region. Mr. Bre, who was a leader in the Piazza Arada Terminal during the fieldwork, mentioned the conflict. "After we started working at *tera*, many *lejoch* (ልጆች, youngsters) got a taste for money, and there was fighting between groups to occupy each other's *sefer*. It was really serious. Some areas were taken away by a stronger group" (Mr. Bre. 40s. *Tera askebari*. July 10, 2018, Piazza Arada). He mentioned that many youngsters took up this line of work, which later caused significant conflicts as they tried to take over others' areas.

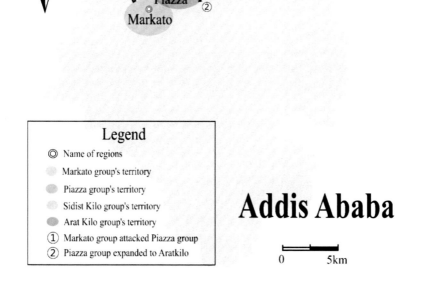

Figure 20. Territorial conflict of *tera askebari* groups in the 1990s

Sometimes, due to a vacancy of a leader in the terminal, some *tera askebari* groups were able to opportunistically expand their territories to other terminals. In the late 1990s, due to the power vacuum at the Arat Kilo Terminal, the Piazza group expanded its territory to the Arat Kilo Terminal. Mr. Yohannes in the Shiromeda Terminal referred to the conflict between group members in Arat Kilo in the late 1990s. "The Arat Kilo group was one of the strongest. However, there was a severe rift among the members, and two of the leaders were assassinated in the middle of the fighting, and those boys split. The *tera askebari* who are working these days are not the real ones" (Mr. Yohannes. 40s. *Tera askebari*. July 11, 2018, Shiromeda Terminal). Based on Mr. Yohannes' narratives, the Arat Kilo group was disbanded because of internal conflict among the members. This created a new possibility for a nearby group in Piazza, only 1.1 km away. "After the Arat Kilo *lejoch* was disbanded, the Piazza *lejoch* expanded their power to Arat Kilo as well as Sidist Kilo" (Mr. Kassahun. 50s. *Tera askebari*. Piazza Arada Terminal). One group in Piazza managed to usurp the business in Arat Kilo Terminal in the absence of a proper ruler, enabling them to seize the nearby Sidist Kilo Terminal as well.

Creation of the *tera askebari* by social projects

The majority of the *tera askebari* grew from street groups from the late 1980s to the 2010s. However, other types of *tera askebari* did not originate in street groups. Two arose from certain projects created to solve social problems.: the first, to reintegrate Eritrean–Ethiopian war veterans, and the second, to involve street children in the city beautification movement.

Designation of Eritrean–Ethiopian war veterans to tera askebari

At the end of the Eritrean–Ethiopian war, the Ethiopian government initiated several projects—some of which included working as a *tera askebari*—to provide employment for discharged soldiers. The Eritrean–Ethiopian war was a conflict that took place between the borders of the two countries from 1998 to 2000. After about 60 years of Italian rule and occupation of the British Administration on behalf of the Allied Forces from 1890 to 1952, Eritrea's territory was annexed to Ethiopia by a United Nations' (UN) decision in 1952. However, the experience of Italy's colonialism had already formed in the Eritreans a strong identity and a moral detachment from Ethiopia (Gilkes 2003: 165-166). This led the Eritreans from 1960 to 1991 to persistently argue for the independence movement against the Imperial Ethiopian Government, the kingdom of Emperor Haile Selassie, and the socialist regime of Mengistu Hailemariam. The Eritrean People's Liberation Front, which began to take over parts of the country in the mid-1970s, took complete control of Eritrea on May 24, 1991. After winning an overwhelming majority of 99.8% in the Eritrean referendum for independence in 1993, they were granted independence under the approval of the UN Observer Mission to Verify the Referendum in Eritrea (UNOVER), achieving full independence on May 24, 1993 (Fikrejesus 2018).

After seven years during which Ethiopia and Eritrea maintained peace, conflicts again arose because of the disputed national boundary issue. There were three border treaties between Eritrea (Italian ruled) and Ethiopia in 1900, 1902, and 1908, none of which were properly delimited or demarcated. Furthermore, the Italian occupation of Ethiopia from 1936 to 1941 made the border issue redundant, which made a marginal difference when the disputed area was administered (Negash & Tronvoll 2000). After independence, the Italian map, created in 1934, argued the Eritreans, should be the basis of the boundary—an assertion not only contrary to international law and treaties, but also unacceptable to Ethiopia (Abbink 1998: 555). The tension between the two countries increased. In May 1998, there was a petit border dispute between local Tigrayan militia and Eritrean soldiers near the Badme region, killing several Eritreans. On May 6, 1998, a vengeful Eritrean unit occupied the Badme area within the Ethiopian border. This prompted a declaration of war by Ethiopia, which caused both numerous casualties and societal damage to both countries.

After the war, about 158,000 Ethiopian soldiers were demobilized, and the necessity of reintegrating them into society was determined. The Ethiopian government requested assistance from the World Bank for a program to support discharged soldiers, which they commenced as an Emergency Demobilization and Reintegration Project (EDRP). By supporting the reintegration of demobilized veterans into society, rehabilitating and reconstructing the infrastructure, and assisting the return of displaced civilians and deportees, the EDRP project was intended to comprehensively finance a post-war recovery program (World Bank 2007). It provided several services—such as apprenticeship, financial support, agricultural assistance, and micro-projects—to integrate veterans into society (Independent Evaluation Group [IEG] 2008). The project also hired in the form of contractual employment in the public sector for jobs such as guards, construction workers, or drivers (Colletta et al. 1996: 58). In all, it hired around 39,330 in contractual employment, and the *tera askebari* was one of the public sector employment options.

Discharged veterans were hired by the government as part of the reintegration program. However, it seems that for veterans, working as *tera askebari* was not a long-term solution. They received a small salary, the work was often short-term, and they had to deal with former gangster *tera askebari* (Colletta et al. 1996: 58).

> One *tera askebari* said:
>> *"There was an Eritrean war in 1991 (by the Ethiopian Calendar). When the young people who returned to their home country from this war suffered unemployment, the government made them work as tera askebari. Their salaries were very low, and most of the soldiers who returned home quit halfway through because tera askebari who had been working for a long time had the actual power" (Mr. Bre. 40s. Tera askebari. July 10, 2018, Piazza Arada).*

During my research, I found one man who had survived in the job until the present day. Mr. Abiyot, a *tera askebari* near the Abune Petros memorial square,[7] was a former veteran *tera askebari*. He was working in the C platform, as shown in Figure 21.[8] When I visited the terminal, he was noting down the *targa* (ታርጋ, plate number) of the minibuses in order, pressing his workers to oversee the minibuses properly. He introduced himself as an ex-combatant who had participated in the Ethiopia–Eritrean war. He said he could not get a proper job after the war, adding that the government had suggested that he work as a *tera askebari*.

> Mr. Abiyot continued:
>> *"After finishing the battle (Eritrean–Ethiopian war), I could not get a proper job. The government recommended that I start tera askebari work, and I was deployed in the center of Piazza" (Mr. Abiyot. 40s. Tera askebari. July 19, 2018, Abune Petros).*

He related how he was initially designated to the center of the Piazza Terminal at Platform F. However, even though he was appointed as "official *tera askebari*" by the government, the former *tera askebari* who had already established their power in that area were not well-disposed toward his working in this capacity. The continuous threats from street youths who had been controlling the business became a major cause of veteran *tera askebari* quitting their jobs.

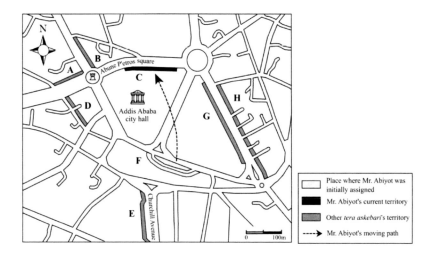

Figure 21. Minibus *tera* near Piazza and Petros (in the time of 2017)

Mr. Abiyot said that he could not bear the power game, which had caused him to move from F *tera* to C *tera*, which was located only 200 meters away from where he had formerly worked. As shown in Table 5, the F *tera* possessed more minibus routes profitable to the *tera askebari* than other routes.

> "Many of them (the former veterans) stopped working in mid-employment. My idea was to start tera askebari work in this area (C tera). I received 25 santim (ሳንቲም, cents)[9] per one taxi in the early days. Many gangsters tried to take over my area so I fought a lot. The situations in the other areas were similar. One person was even killed in Sidist Kilo (Mr. Abiyot)."

He mentioned that holding on to this work was not an easy job; however, he fought and was able to defend his territory. After working for more than 15 years, he formed a group with his acquaintances and worked as a legal operator. The formalization of his group gave him the justification to reign over the area, and he maintained that the fighting in the territory had ceased and the area was now peaceful.

The Eritrean–Ethiopian war veterans' engagement with the *tera askebari*

business was an attempt to reintegrate them into society by providing them with
work opportunities in the minibus terminal. However, this program did not have a
conspicuous influence. Because the program was poorly managed and the former
tera askebari insisted on their business rights, most of the veteran *tera askebari*
resigned midway. The only way for them to survive in this vicious street business
was to follow Mr. Abiyot's example and become a *gulbetegna* to maintain control
over their *tera*.

Table 5. Minibus routes of each platform in the Piazza Terminal

Platform	Operating routes
A	Autobus Tera At'ena Tera
B	Asko Rufael
C	Menelik - Jalmeda - Ferensay Menelik - Shiromeda
D	T'orhailoch Ayer T'ena
E	Stadium - Dembel - Bole Michael - Bole Stadium - Lancha - Gotera - Saris - Adey Abeba - Kaliti Akaki Mexico - K'era Mexico - Jemo Michael - Jemo
F	Ras desta Rufael Shegole Addis sefer Pawlos Medhanealem Winget Berchiko fabrika Asko
G	Stadium - Gotera - Saris - K'aliti Stadium - Bole Mexico
H	British Embassy - Megenagna - Kara - Yeka Abado Semen Hotel - Adisu Gebeya - Sululta Haya Hulet - Kazanchis Chilot - Medhanialem

Source: Author's own observation from fieldwork, July 2018.

Tera askebari created by Gash Abera Molla's city beautification movement

The other type of *tera askebari* was created by one singer's social project. Gash Abera Molla, a successful Ethiopian singer and *krar* (hረር, Ethiopian style lyre with five to six strings) player living in the United States, made a contribution to the formation of the *tera askebari*. His original name was Seleshi Demissie, but his nickname—adopted when he took on an initiative to beautify the urban environment—was based on one of the main characters of his songs, Gash Abera, an old man who took care of his community (Shelemay 2009: 3). In 1998, after spending 20 years in the United States, Gash Abera Molla returned to Addis Ababa. During his visit, he realized that his childhood memories and the images he had of the city did not match the realities he saw. He was appalled by the litter scattered in the streets and the huge number of beggars, unemployed youth, and homeless people struggling to survive.

Gash Abera Molla, starred at one TV show and talked about what he felt and why he initiated the project:

> *"The city was dirty and messed up in those days. When I saw Piazza, it was dark, everywhere was a place to pee on the roadside, and garbage and waste were thrown everywhere! If you had seen Addis Ababa itself, it was most disgusting to pass through that area. Even when you went into the compound of the vegetable market, all the garbage from this market was thrown in front of it. There was a taxi tera there, all the worn-out clothes were sold there, every electric pole was a place to pee under, garbage was thrown there too. In the name of the holy father!"* (Gash Abera Molla. Interview at Enchawawot. Season 9, by the Ethiopian Broadcasting Service. August 26, 2018. Translated by the author).

The reality that he witnessed motivated him to establish, in late 1998, the Gash Abera Molla Foundation to address social and environmental problems in his home country (Nita 2001; Nebiyu 2015: 95-102). He set up an urban environmental improvement project by involving unemployed and young people to work on solid waste disposal and urban beautification. About 13,000 street children were mobilized to help clean up the city (UNICEF 2002: 29). The project was influential in that almost everyone from this corner of the city cooperated in the project, which was covered by several foreign media (Meaza 2016: 10-11). The widespread media coverage advertised *tera askebari*'s activities to the citizens of Addis Ababa.

As part of the project, many street youths were appointed as *tera askebari* to guide minibuses and passengers. "It was Gash Abera Molla who created the *tera askebari* work" (*Tera askebari* at Kara Station. 40s. male. July 21, 2018). "There was a man called Gash Abera Molla, and he gave shifts to the street children for the first time" (*Tera askebari* at Ttorhailoch Station. 40s. male July 24, 2018). The influence of this project made a vivid impression on the citizens and current *tera askebari*.

Tera askebari as a community leader

2005 Ethiopian general election and tera askebari's role

The 2005 Ethiopian general election was the first election that freely allowed opposition parties to conduct campaigns. In the former elections, held in 1991 and 2000, the ruling Ethiopian People's Revolutionary Democratic Front (EPRDF) used oppressive means, such as monitoring voters and suppressing the campaigns of opposition parties, to seize power (Abbink 2000: 157). By contrast, the positively conducted 2005 election allowed opposition parties to deliver speeches and distribute their programs. In this free atmosphere, the Addis Ababa city invited both the ruling and the main opposition parties—EPRDF and Coalition for Unity and Democracy (CUD)—to host the large mass rallies, attended by in excess of an estimated one million people (Balsvik 2007: 168). It was the first election that allowed people to express their political choices, and this unprecedented experience led citizens to have high expectations in democratic elections.

However, the ruling party was concerned that the opposition parties would take more seats in the House of Peoples' Representatives than expected. On the eve of the voting day, Prime Minister Meles Zenawi declared a state of emergency, including a one-month ban on public demonstrations and outdoor gatherings (Aalen & Tronvoll 2009: 195). On June 4, 2005, the election result was postponed from June 8 by a month, amidst numerous deceptions and vote rigging (Balsvik 2007: 172). After the election, the government delayed the counting process, eventually releasing the results after three weeks. The CUD argued that the government had deliberately delayed the counting so as to manipulate the results (Aalen & Tronvoll 2009: 195). Unofficial reports stated that opposition parties would take the majority, but the preliminary result showed that the ruling party had done so: EPRDF won 320 seats, while opposition parties won around 200 seats (Carter Center 2009: 4). Rumors and suspicions proliferated, and many people believed that the election result had been manipulated.

This evoked a furious reaction from the students. On June 6, the Addis Ababa University students defied a government ban on demonstrations and held a peaceful sit-in demonstration against the compromised integrity of the election (The New York Times 2005). It was so violently suppressed that the protesters were beaten with batons. During the confrontation, one female student was killed, sparking extensive protest throughout the country. On June 8, students flooded to the street and continued the protest in the center of the city, in Mexico area (ECADF 2011). Here at least 36 people died and 100 were wounded (Lyons 2006: 2). The student movement also inspired the minibus drivers and citizens to riot. Taxi drivers participated in strikes from June 6 to 8. The demonstrations continued for three days. During this period, the security forces and local administrators had threatened to revoke the taxi drivers' licenses if they did not resume business (Al jazeera 2005). Other demonstrators stopped rioting only after they had been severely beaten and threatened by the local authorities.

During this confusion, it was the *tera askebari* who played a leading role in pacifying the demonstrators. The *tera askebari* initially participated in the strike, along with minibus drivers. However, they later changed their position as regulators of the strike action. Amidst the confusion, the local administrators approached the *tera askebari* and asked them to take conciliatory action to control the demonstrators and stop the riots. The *tera askebari* appealed to many taxi drivers to restart their transport service, returned many demonstrators to their homes, and restarted their business. There was a benefit for the *tera askebari* by allying with the government (Di Nunzio 2014: 452). The *tera askebari*'s alliance with the ruling party in the 2005 crisis further helped them to consolidate their ties with the ruling party and strengthen their power in the street economy.

Promotion of community policing and the role of tera askebari

During the massive riots of the 2005 election, the government was surprised by the mass youth gathering. Considering the participation of unemployed youth to be the cause of the 2005 demonstration, the government engaged in community policing activities through youth associations and registered some *tera askebari* as agents for community policing.

The youth association, which is a major institution of community policing, has existed since the *Derg* regime, at the end of which the Addis Ababa Youth

Association (AAYA) was established in 1998 (NAMATI 2021). However, after the 2005 election, the government, seeking to strengthen the linkage with the youth, established new associations, and expanded former ones. In mid-2006, the government formulated the Youth Development Package (YDP)—targeting both rural and urban youth— with the aim of helping them make proper decisions (Eyob 2009: 28). The government, in an attempt to strengthen the relationship with the urban youth, established a tri-partite platform—that is, the Addis Ababa Youth Forum, the Addis Ababa Women's Forum, and the Addis Ababa Inhabitant's Forum (AAIF)—where youth could engage and participate in politics. In August 2007 and February 2009, the government also organized the National Youth Conference, which was celebrated by more than 7,000 people (Eyob 2009: 26-28). Although these institutions' objectives show little differences, the ruling party's major goal in expanding the youth community was to coerce youths to their sides and extend their influence to the grassroots.

The promotion of the youth league aimed to expand the ruling party's influence among the youth, and principally to expand the surveillance network through youth agents to police the community. Community policing is defined as people's engagement in providing policing services to the community, particularly to places where the police could not reach. It includes collecting information about suspicious political activities in communities (Di Nunzio 2014: 445). It is explicitly mentioned as one of the youth association's goals— "alleviating the socio-economic problem of youth unemployment and anti-social involvements of the youths" (AAYA 2021).

The government intervened in the *tera askebari* specifically to recruit them as one of their agents. According to the fieldwork in 2017 and 2018, three *tera askebari*, one from Bole Bras Terminal, and two from Piazza Arada Terminal, related that, when they tried to register their groups into the Micro and Small Enterprises agency (MES agency), the government asked them to register with the AAYA. They described how it was their duty to inform the police about any crime or suspicious activities. For the government, by hiring several *tera askebari* to their side, they could extend their surveillance to the grassroots of society. For the *tera askebari*, their involvement in the government's community policing scheme extended their role of traffic controllers to para-police, supervising the community from terminals to the larger grassroots of society. This elevated the position of the *tera askebari* as prominent figures in traffic management and as a security force with the backing of political power.

The rise and expansion of *tera askebari*

Under the development of the city, the number of minibuses rapidly increased, with various accompanying social challenges emerging around the minibus terminal. Inadequate road parking for minibuses often caused congestion, particularly during peak hours (Kumar & Barrett 2008: 2). Fierce competition among minibus operators touting their business was often overheated, as each of them rushed to out-compete each other and collect passengers faster (Fekadu 2013: 69). As there were no rules on how to line up, passengers often cut in lines or boarded in a disorderly manner. Furthermore, the disorder in these terminals gave rise to social problems, such as robberies and pickpocketing. This situation was exacerbated by the absence of control towers and regulations from the government side of the minibus business. After privatization in the 1980s, the sector was left unregulated by the government, and traffic regulations on minibus operations did not exist, leading the minibuses to operate on any route until the introduction of the new traffic agency in 2009 (Tilahun 2014: 123). While the need for traffic management was clearly urgent, the city government and minibus associations did not intervene to control this situation.

Under these conditions, it was *tera askebari* who participated in controlling the situation. In the early days, the *tera askebari* business was a means of collecting money for a few street groups. Many *tera askebari* leaders who worked in the early days argued that the work was just a simple task of organizing passengers; one *tera askebari* recounted, "At that time, I earned a few *santim* from minibus operators when I arranged the passengers" (Mr. Kassahun (50s years). *Tera askebari*. July 10, 2018, Piazza Arada). However, the increasing chaos and social problems soon required more specialized behavior from the *tera askebari*. Instead of simply collecting tolls, they adopted various management methods, such as controlling the order of the minibuses and assisting the passengers. They also started to take charge of policing activities in the terminal. "If we found a thief, we could hand them over to police. Sometimes, we simply caught them and scolded them" (*Tera askebari* at Mexico Terminal, July 24, 2018). Together with this process, the idea of collecting tolls in the territory was adopted by the local influential people, which led to the expansion of *tera askebari* business throughout the city.

The emergence of the *tera askebari*'s activities in controlling the minibuses was a welcome introduction for many citizens, as the disorder among the minibuses decreased to an extent. "Before the *tera askebari* started their work, taking a *taxi* (minibus) was like a war. I have also lost mobile phones when getting in it" (Mr. Michael. 20s. Passenger. June 23, 2017, Gerji Mabrat Hail Terminal). Under the rapid expansion of minibus services, the lack of a management system by minibus operators and the government's indifference in providing public services led to the rise and development of *tera askebari* in Addis Ababa. The government's failure to meet public demands led to the emergence of the *tera askebari* to exercise public dominance on the ground, and their business has expanded together with the city's growth.

Summary

This chapter aimed to explore the process of the development of the *tera askebari* in the urban transport sector by recounting their history. The *Tera askebari* were created sporadically by street youth from the late 1980s to the 2010s. Their business operation method was based on their power over minibus operators, in which their thuggish, violent actions paved the way for the collection of tolls. Sometimes, power struggles surfaced between street groups to take over other *tera askebari* business, as it was a lucrative pursuit. This series of *tera askebari* dominance over the street economy can also be understood as an Ethiopian context, in which the traditional notion of power and authority, in which one person is constrained to obey the orders from above, has been transformed into new forms in which principally male, strong figures could exert street power. This was the background against which the *tera askebari* were able to sustain their power in the minibus business.

In the 1990s, a new type of *tera askebari* has emerged in the city, which are created by social projects. The first was the *tera askebari* designated for the Eritrean–Ethiopian war veterans to integrate them into society. It was a first form of government-hired type of *tera askebari*, but it did not have a conspicuous influence as many of the veterans resigned midway. The second was the *tera askebari* created by the famous singer called Gash Abera Molla. As part of his city beautification project, many street youths were appointed as *tera askebari* to guide minibuses and passengers. This activity was covered by various media, which enabled *tera askebari*'s activities to become known to the citizens.

The *Tera askebari* also had an influence as community leaders. In 2005, when a massive demonstration occurred protesting the fraud of the general election, the *tera askebari* played a crucial role. Initially, they participated in the strike and demonstration, but changed their position to that of regulators when the ruling party made conciliatory approaches to them. After this, the *tera askebari* took a leading role in pacifying the demonstrators and forcing minibus workers to return to their businesses. Their power grew in the street economy as they became involved in the government's community policing scheme. This extended their role of traffic controllers to that of para-police, supervising the community from terminals to the larger grassroots of society. Through this development, the *tera askebari* rose in status from being a prominent force in traffic management to becoming a security force backed by political power.

Through urban development, the minibus business expanded rapidly and various social challenges emerged around the minibus terminals—such as cutting in line, boarding in a disorderly manner, overheated touting, robberies, and pickpocketing. While the need for control of the minibuses was widely apparent, the city government simply made no attempt to control this situation. Under these conditions, youths who were residing around the newly-created minibus terminals initiated the *tera askebari* work by controlling the problems. Like the initial *tera askebari*, they claimed territorial rights and extracted tolls from the minibus workers. Their activities were no longer confined to those of queue keepers, but had extended to those of guide and provider of security to the citizens as well. Despite their informal activities which were not carried out with fixed methods, the *tera askebari* were those who gave guidelines for citizens and minibuses in the minibus terminals. Through the process whereby the citizens' demands for minibus management and the spread of the *tera askebari* influenced each other, the *tera askebari*'s activities were consolidated as a necessary service in the transport sector in Addis Ababa.

Notes

[1] The *Derg* ruled Ethiopia from 1974 to 1987 until the leader Mengistu Haile Mariam transferred administrative power to civilians in 1987. Later, the new government—the People's Democratic Republic of Ethiopia (PDRE)—began to run the country, but it was *de facto* ruled by the former *Derg* members and adhered to the socialist ideology. The socialist regime presided over Ethiopia was from 1974 to 1991.

[2] The minibus service began during the *Derg* period. In the 1980s, used minibuses were imported from the Soviet Union in large quantities and painted blue/white to distinguish them from ordinary Bongo bus.

[3] "Mengistu Haile Mariam imported the minibuses and provided the service for 10 years; after that, he announced that anyone could start a minibus business" (Mr. Dengelu. 72 years old, conducted through an informant. Former minibus driver. October 22, 2020, At'ena Tera Terminal).

[4] Mengistu Haile Mariam was a leader as well as president of the socialist regime of Ethiopia from 1974 to 1991.

[5] Etymologically, *gulbet* (ጉልበት) refers to a knee, strength, power, energy, or vigor (Kane 1990. vol 2: 1889-1890), and the term *gulbetegna* means a strong and powerful person or one who does not tire and can endure hardships. The word *gulbet* is used to describe humans as well as things (for instance, *yemekina gulbet*, የመኪና ጉልበት: vehicle's power, such as an engine's ability). *Gulbet* can also indicate physical aspects (for instance, *yegulbet sra*, የጉልበት ስራ: physical labor or *yegulbet waga*, የጉልበት ዋጋ: labor cost).

[6] According to Mr. Mamo (40s), who was currently working at the Arat Kilo Terminal, the *tera askebari* at Arat Kilo appeared in 1985.

[7] The memorial was built to honor Abune Petros, Ethiopian Orthodox Bishop, who was martyred by the fascist Italians.

[8] Platform was called *tera* among the *tera askebari*, which refers to territory or specific area.

[9] 1 USD was equivalent to 8 Ethiopian birr in June 2000. Searched at <https://www.investing.com/currencies/usd-etb-historical-data>

Chapter 4. State Intervention and the Current Practice of *Tera Askebari*: Case of Group Y at Platform X

Introduction

Since the 1990s, there has been a wide recognition of Micro and Small Enterprises (MSEs) and their contribution to economic growth in developing countries. MSEs have been regarded to play an important role in solving poverty and unemployment among urban people as it provides an important income source (Wolday 2016: 94). Thus, supporting of MSEs has received attention in development settings due to its potential to bolster economic growth and improve the livelihoods of the poor (Harper & Finnegan 1998: 7-9).

In Addis Ababa, about 40% of the urban labor force engaged in MSEs activities, with 60% of the national economy consisting of informal activities (CSA 2003; Rahel & Issac 2010: 234). In 2011, the Addis Ababa city government launched an MSEs development program to solve the burgeoning problems in urban areas, especially urban poverty and unemployment. This program also aimed to register unemployed individuals and workers of MSEs who had previously worked informally. Like many other informal works, such as shoe-shiner, parking attendants, and street vendors, involve in the MSEs program, it was not an exception to *tera askebari*.

Tera askebari, groups of people who manage minibuses and passengers at the minibus terminal, have played an important role in the management of the urban transport sector since the late 1980s. Since 2011 when the MSEs program has launched, most early *tera askebari* groups in the city registered to the program under the slogan of formalization. However, despite the number of studies on MSEs program in Addis Ababa, there have been no studies investigating on the current practice of *tera askebari* after the MSEs program intervene to them.[1]

This chapter focuses on the dynamics between state and current practice of *tera askebari*, especially focusing on how the boss of *tera askebari* group (*wanna*) utilize the benefits of regulatory environment. Accordingly, there are three research questions that I attempt to answer in this chapter. First, how does the government intervene to the *tera askebari*? Second, what are the characteristics of MSEs policy? Third, what kind of employment features does the *wanna* shows in the form of utilizing the MSEs program?

The study was based on fieldwork in 2019. The research was conducted in the eastern center of Addis Ababa, Megenagna Terminal. Within this terminal, I focused my research on the southeastern part, which I am going to call Platform X (refer to Figure 4 in page 10). This chapter starts with a brief introduction to the MSEs program in Addis Ababa. Next, I describe the process of government intervention in *tera askebari*. Following that, I will describe my observations of the management activities of one of the groups, specifically of their income structure and hiring system. Finally, I will conclude the chapter by demonstrating the implications of *tera askebari*'s activities. In this chapter, I allocated a code, an abbreviation form of their status and ID, to the workers; for example, *Wanna* A is expressed as *Wanna*-A, Manager A is expressed as Mgr-A, and Young Boy A is expressed as YB-A. Minibus drivers and attendants have not been included in the current analysis.

Outline of the MSEs program

Aim of the MSEs program

Ethiopia has launched various development initiatives and policies to promote national economic growth. From the end of the 1990s, the Ethiopian government has paid heed to the MSEs development as they constituted the second-largest employment-generating sector in Ethiopia (CSA 2005). Unlike other countries that target small and medium enterprises (SMEs), the Ethiopian government has focused on a lower level of business, i.e., micro and small enterprises. Supporting and developing of MSEs has been regarded as an important way to reduce poverty and solve unemployment, which can further accelerate economic growth and contribute towards the achievement of industrialization in the long run (Berihu et al. 2014: 9; Arega et al. 2016: 581).

The initial government policy to develop MSEs was introduced in 1998 by the Federal Micro and Small Enterprises Development Agency (FeMSEDA) through the Proclamation no. 33/98. Following that, the Regional Micro and Small Enterprises[2] Development Agencies (ReMSEDAs) were launched in 2004/05[2] to provide extension service to the regional zones and *woreda* (ወረዳ, district office).[3] Addis Ababa City launched an independent department called Addis Ababa Job Opportunity Creation and Enterprise Development Bureau (from here, MSEs development agency or MSEs agency) and installed its bureaus in each of the *woreda* and sub-cities to extend its service to the citizens.

The MSEs development agency in Addis Ababa launched a program which targets the unemployed individuals and informal workers (see Wolday 2016: 95).

The program aimed to create job opportunities and support MSEs to move to a higher business level. The core objective of the program has been described as follows: "The primary objective of the strategy framework was to create a favorable environment for MSE development and to provide a more targeted policy support to MSEs so that MSEs could facilitate economic growth, create long-term jobs, strengthen cooperation between MSEs, provide the basis for medium and large-scale enterprises and promote export" (Berihu et al. 2014: 1). Thus, a major goal of this program was to develop MSEs to the maturity stage, so that they possess competitiveness and achieve high profits, which would help them to move to a higher stage.

Characteristics of the program

One of the major characteristics of the program was that the main agents who initiated the project were people, not the government. As "create the job by yourself,"[4] a motto of MSEs policy presents, those who want to start work should make a group and register it in the MSEs agency. The MSEs program promotes collective participation at the local level, so the groups should be organized with residents who belong to the same *woreda* (Chinigò 2019: 84-85). Following that, each of the group visits the MSEs agency in the *woreda* and propose their future business ideas to it.

People can register into two types of enterprises, that is individual and union. Individual is operated individually, and in the case of union-type organization, 6 up to 30 people could enroll on one enterprise. In union-type organization, the role and responsibilities of the leaders, secretary, auditor and members are stated. The *tera askebari* business was a union-type, which can be enrolled only with multiple members.

The enterprises were defined into micro or small enterprises according to their assets. Table 6 presents the definition of MSEs in Ethiopia, which was announced by FeMSEDA in 2011. Microenterprises refer to firms that have a maximum of five employees and whose total assets are less than or equal to 100,000 *birr* if operating in the industrial sector or that of 50,000 *birr* if operating in the service sector.[5] Small enterprises refer to firms that have 6 to 30 employees and whose total assets are lesser than 1,500,000 *birr* if operating in the industrial sector or that of 500,000 *birr* if operating in the service sector.

Table 6. Definition of micro and small enterprise in Ethiopia

Type of enterprise	Sector	Human power	Total asset (*birr*)
Micro enterprise	Industry	≤ 5	$\leq 100,000$
	Service	≤ 5	$\leq 50,000$
Small enterprise	Industry	6-30	$\leq 1,500,000$
	Service	6-30	$\leq 500,000$

Source: FeMSEDA (2011)

Each enterprise was required to create a bank account for the group which was directly linked to the agency of MSEs. When they save, 10% of their savings will be saved as their group's assets, 5% is deducted as tax, and 85% is considered as private savings which the group members can use freely for their personal use. While enterprises were encouraged to save their earnings regularly, this was not a mandatory condition.

Each enterprises' assets and achievements were evaluated every six months, which was to determine the development status of the enterprises. The development status was divided into start-up stage, growth stage, expansion stage, and maturity stage. At the start-up stage, the government provides training support related to business management and production techniques, or provides loans that continue up to the expansion stage.

Tera askebari's participation to the MSEs program

Governments intervention attempt before MSEs program

Addis Ababa experienced a high rate of urbanization, which impacted the development of public transportation. With the increase in the necessities to control minibuses, the business of *tera askebari* has also expanded in the city. Meanwhile, the government was not satisfied with the informally working *tera askebari* in the whole city, so they attempted to intervene in the *tera askebari* to seize their business. According to the interview, the government suggested several *tera askebari* to be employed as full-time workers. However, most of the *tera askebari* rejected this idea.

One *tera askebari* at Semit Terminal mentioned:

> *"We started the work by ourselves 10 years ago. Initially, there were few peoples who had power, like us. However, the government tried to take our work consecutively. Once, they came to us and asked us if we wanted to be fully employed, but we rejected. Why? Because if they fully hire us, we know that we will get lesser money than what we are earning now. It was us who initiated the work! We fought so many times to keep this work and keep the order in the terminal"* (Mr. Beyene. 30s. Tera askebari. July 8, 2017, Semit Terminal).

Many *tera askebari*, who have gone through hardships to keep their business, were not satisfied with the government's suggestions. As the idea to control minibuses was their own idea, they perceived that the government was simply trying to take away their properties. In addition, the *tera askebari* knew that they would earn much less if they were hired by the government. For example, the one-month salary of the lowest-level civil servant in 2005 was around 1,000 *birr*,[6] an amount that they can easily earn by just working for three hours. Also, many of them would mostly work part-time, permitting them to adjust their personal schedules to suit their needs. Thus, cooperation with the government did not carry any merits for them. Instead of being subordinated and losing their profitable source of income, the *tera askebari* rejected the government's suggestions and did not hand over their business.

Tera askebari's participation in the MSEs program

Unlike previous attempts that have failed to involve the *tera askebari*'s participation, the government has achieved success in drawing *tera askebari* through the MSEs development project, due to the overall structural changes. In 2011, the Addis Ababa government launched the MSEs development agency to extend its control over unregulated enterprises. Civil servants went out to the street and persuaded informal workers to work legally to register their business information with the district administration (*woreda*). This was a large-scale process, with there being 1.5 million people joining in four years since the embarkment of the MSEs program (Ministry of Urban Development & Housing 2016: 10). Accordingly, enforcement has become heightened, and those who do not have formal licenses have become targets of securities.[7] Therefore, most of the informal workers in the streets, such as shoe shiners, parking guards, and street vendors, as well as *tera askebari* have started to register their businesses with the MSEs program to operate legally.

Working condition

In the early days of the program, the *woreda* offices suggested *tera askebari* to operate their business with certain rules. First, *tera askebari* were suggested to issue a ticket and collect the designated amount of service charge. *Tera askebari* at Semit and Mexico Terminal mentioned that the government distributed a ticket to *tera askebari* to ensure the better management of minibuses, and they were recommended to collect 1.25 *birr* per minibus.[8]

Second, they were suggested to leave the work in a certain period of time. The MSEs program's major aim was to develop the economic level of the MSEs and enhance their competitiveness in the market. Thus, MSEs were suggested to increase their assets by saving their daily earnings to their group's bank account. When MSEs register their groups into the program, they were obliged to set up a goal, such as a savings target and their business plan after the programs over. *Tera askebari* groups were same. They had a set period to develop their business, which was different depending on the contract they made with the *woreda* office. In the case of *tera askebari* group in T'orhailoch Terminal, they were required to leave the work in five years. In the case of *tera askebari* group in Bole Bras Terminal, it was four years[9] and the *tera askebari* at Semit Terminal was three years.[10]

Third, they had to save their earnings in their respective bank accounts, which is linked to the MSEs agency. As aforesaid, each enterprise was required to create a bank account for the group which was directly linked to the agency of MSEs. When they save, 10% of their savings will be saved as their group's assets, 5% is deducted as tax, and 85% is considered as private savings which the group members can use freely for their personal use. Each group made contract with their affiliated *woreda* office, so their obligatory savings were different by the groups (Figure 22).

In the case of Sidist Kilo Groups, which works 50 meters east to the Yekatit 12 Square, had to save 200 *birr* a day. In the case of Shiromeda Group, which was running their business near traditional clothes Shiromeda Market, they needed to save 300 *birr* a day. In the case of Piazza Group, their obligation was higher than the aforementioned two groups, in which they were required to save 1,200 *birr* per day. In the case of Faransai Group, they mentioned that the saving was not obligation but recommendation, and the members of the group save 50 *birr* per day by their own wills. Meanwhile, some groups were suggested to save their earnings in a longer period. Groups at Kara Terminal argued that they are obliged to save 6,000 *birr* a month, while the Arat Kilo Group, which run in the eastern part of the Arat Kilo Roundabout, argued that they had to save 100,000 *birr* a year.

Figure 22. Bank account of one *tera askebari* group

Reality after the registration to MSEs program

Despite the earlier working condition, *tera askebari*'s business started to show different aspects after the registration. First, the 1.25 *birr* ticketing service did not last long. Amid the busy working schedule, *tera askebari* found it inconvenient to issue a ticket and manage the minibus simultaneously. Eventually, *tera askebari* halted to utilize this system and turned back to the former way of management, as like one *tera askebari* at Mexico Terminal said it as a "boring system."[11] Second, despite the pledged period, most *tera askebari* groups were running a business over the contracted period. Table 7 presents the MSE program registration years for the *tera askebari* groups that I researched in 2017 and 2018. Depending on the terminal, the year of registration differed between 2011 and 2017. While most of the groups argued that they had a pledged period of contract, it seemed that many groups were still owning the license and running the business in the time of fieldwork. In other words, many *tera askebari* who registered in the early days, were perpetuating their power until the current moment.

Table 7. Registration year of *tera askebari* groups to MSEs program

Name of the terminals	Registration year
Piazza	2011
Megenagna (Inner terminal)	2011
Faransai	2012
Mexico Square (*Sarbet* direction)	2012
Kaliti	2013
Kazanchis	2013
Kolfe	2015
Ttorhailoch	2015
Chilot Adebabay	2017
Salite Meheret	2017

Source: Author's fieldwork in 2017 to 2018.

Lastly, *tera askebari*'s saving practice raised a question on the development possibility of the MSEs program. I would like to observe a saving record of one group, which I am going to call Group G. The group information is concealed in this thesis to not to reveal the personal information. In this group, the number of members were 10 to 15 and the group's daily earning was approximately 6,000 to 8,000 *birr*. Table 8 shows the saving records of Group G from June 2017 to November 2017. The saving category is largely divided into three sections: tax, seed money, and private savings. This group saved for a total of six times from June 12 to November 10, 2017. When they saved their money, 5% was deducted as tax, 10% was saved as seed money for an MSEs program, and 85% was saved as private savings, which the *tera askebari* group could withdraw at any time. As an example of savings on June 12, the group saved 800 *birr* of earnings. Of this amount, 5%, which is 40 *birr*, was deducted as tax. 10% of the amount, which is 80 *birr*, was saved as the group's seed money. After that, 680 *birr* was saved as private savings.

Table 8. Saving records of one *tera askebari* group to group's bank account

Date	Amount*	Tax (5%)		Seed Money (10%)		Private Saving (85%)		
		Saving	Total	Saving	Total	Saving	Withdrawal	Balance
12-Jun-17	800	40	40	80	80	680	0	680
30-Jun-17	2,400	120	160	240	320	2,040	0	2,720
07-Jul-17	3,600	180	340	360	680	3,060	0	5,780
20-Jul-17	2,400	120	460	240	920	2,040	0	7,820
24-Aug-17	7,500	0	0	0	0	0	7,500	320
06-Nov-17	6,000	300	760	600	1,520	5,100	0	5,420
07-Nov-17	3,800	190	950	380	1,900	3,230	0	8,650
10-Nov-17	8,000	0	0	0	0	0	8,000	650
Total			950		1,900	16,150	15,500	650**

Note: This table is compiled based on the actual format of bankbook.
* The Amount includes both savings and withdrawal.
** Total Saving: 19,000 = [Tax: 950 (5%) + Seed Money: 1,900 (10%) + Private Saving: 16,150 (85%)]. Final balance of Private Saving = Private Saving 16,150 - 15,000 = 650.

Within five months period, the group saved six times and withdrew two times. There are two things noticeable. The first is irregular saving practices. In June and July, they saved two times, while they did not save any earnings from August to October. Also, the saving amount is irregular, which ranges from 800 *birr* to 6,000 *birr*. Second, they were not saving the actual amount of the earnings. Aforementioned, the Group G's daily earning was around 6,000 to 8,000 *birr* since they were running the business in a lucrative terminal. Meanwhile, their saving record shows that they did not save their whole earnings but rather save a partial. One member of the Group G mentioned that they prefer to share the daily earnings on that day instead of saving to group account.

Then, what does this phenomenon explain and why *tera askebari* seems to avoid save on group account while the MSEs program seems to be future-promising? The answers could be found on several *tera askebari*'s discourse. The first is high inflation rate. Addis Ababa is one of the most expensive cities to live in Africa in terms of cost living and consumer price (Faria 2022). The country experienced high inflation rate in recent decades. From 2011 to 2019, the average annual inflation rate was 14.03% (World Bank 2022b). To compare, the world average was 2.59% in the same period (World Bank 2022c). Thus, the long-term saving practice does not give them merit as the value of savings and the market price in the future would not same. One *tera askebari* at Autobus Tera argued "We saved for more than six years and now, can you see? One kilogram of potato is 25 *birr*. It was 6 *birr* six years ago. With the saved money, we could buy a new car or already started a new business" (Mr. Tesfaye. 50s. *Tera askebari*. July 19, 2018, Autobus Tera Terminal). Thus, they found no merit to save their money regularly into the MSEs account.

Also, there were high distrust among the *tera askebari* on the transparency of the program. "When we joined the Micro (MSEs development program), the agency said that they will develop our (economic) level if we save 50,000 *birr* every month. Seven years passed but nothing has occurred" (Mr. Ashanafi. 40s. July 24, 2018, Ttorhailoch Terminal). According to Mr. Ashanafi, his groups saved regularly, but nothing has changed and they were never suggested to do other businesses. He continued "Have not the micro (agency) promised us to give us a new level? but the reality is not."

Some *tera askebari* expressed distrust on the MSEs program, arguing that it will bring them a less benefits. Mr. Mehari said, "The reason why micro is really bad institution is that they suggested us to do a chicken farm, coffee shop, but we know that we will earn much less than we start that business!" (Mr. Mehari. 40s.

July 24, 2018, Mexico Terminal). Some *tera askebari* argued that their saved money has "disappeared" in the middle. Based on the argument of the Mr. Bre in Piazza Terminal, they saved around 240,000 *birr* but it was stolen in the middle. When they questioned, the government simply said, "the money has been earned illegally so we cannot give you." The other *tera askebari* at Megenagna terminal argued "We saved 200,000 *birr* only this year. But when we visit the office and ask to withdraw, they refuse. We collected 4,000,000 *birr* until now, but the government erased the record! We know they have a plan to destroy us, but we will never leave here until we get that money" (Mr. Tesfaye. 40s. July 12, 2018, Megenagna Terminal). Thus, based on the uncertainty and the unclearness of the program, many *tera askebari* in the current days showed tendency to save only some part of their daily earnings, and were not passionate to increase their assets, in addition to the MSEs agency's weak involvement.

Tera askebari groups at Megenagna Terminal

History of Megenagna Terminal

Megenagna (መገናኛ) is one of the centers in Addis Ababa, which is located in the Eastern part of the city. Megenagna means communication, confluence, intersection, or junction in Amharic (Leslau 1973; Kane 1990: 343).[12] The place has been named Megenagna, as it has been playing the role of an intersection for a century. The early history of the Megenagna Terminal starts from the era of Menelik II. In the 19th century, Emperor Menelik II founded a capital city in the Hora Finfinne area of the current Oromia region and christened it Addis Ababa. Megenagna did not receive much attention as it was located in the outskirts of the city, but it served as a horse carriage terminal, which helped connect the city and the countryside from an early stage.

As the city developed, the Megenagna Terminal evolved as a hub for public transportation. Although Megenagna was not a major center at that time, it had geographically significant as a link to the countryside, as it connected the center of the city to the eastern edge.[13] Due to its geographical position, Megenagna developed as a platform for public transport called the *anbessa* bus since the 1960s.

> *"In the 1960s when the number of populations was very small, a small number of taxies and vehicles were there in general. The price of taxies and buses was also cheap, of course, the value of*

*the money was high. For example, Megenagna to Piazza bus was
15 santim, the taxi was 25 santim.[14] Anbessa bus no. 6 was
assigned in Megenagna. The routine was from Lamberet to
Megenagna and then to Piazza and Merkato. It was not a form of
the terminal but was just a small area on the roadside. There were
not many buildings. The big portion of the area was covered with
forest, except the narrow asphalt road which passes from Kotebe to
Piazza. We were able to see a car coming from Piazza side to here
from a kilometer away. we used to play football on foot narrow
road as the car passes rarely" (Resident of Megenagna area, 75
years old, male, September 21, 2020).*

The above is an extract from the narration of a gentleman who had spent his
life in Megenagna since the 1960s. According to him, the Megenagna Terminal
was a small platform at which public buses would stop. The major terminal, at
that time, in the eastern part was the Lamberet Terminal, located 1.2 km east of
Megenagna, which served the intercity bus service.

It was around the mid-2000s that Megenagna have developed into an
important city terminal. In the early 2000s, this terminal was operated with only a
Higer bus that operated a long-distance route and an *anbessa* bus. However, due
to population growth and an increase in demand for transportation, Megenagna
started operating transport services to various destinations. Additionally, the
government's highway construction projects influenced the development of the
terminal. The construction of the Ring Road in 2004, which directly links the
Megenagna to the southern part of the city, bolstered the development of the
terminal (see Mo et al. 2008: 3).[15] "This crowded Megenagna hasn't been like this
before, years back there was a small terminal which was only allowed for *anbessa*
city buses and buses called *k'et'e k'et'e*. But later on, like eight years ago, the
terminal has widened and allowed to other midi-buses and minibuses. It seems
that the crowd gets bigger every single day" (Mr. Dani. 30s. Minibus attendant.
September 20, 2020). Based on Mr. Dani's narrative, who has worked as a
minibus attendant for 10 years, the Megenagna Terminal seems to have
experienced rapid development recently. The increasing number of passengers
and the need for transportation pressured minibus services to start operating from
the mid-2000s, which has led to the development of Megenagna as a major
terminal in this metropolis.

Megenagna Terminal at present

Currently, Megenagna is a major city center in Addis Ababa. It is a commercial area for businessmen and street vendors, a recreation center, and a rendezvous point for citizens, as it houses various facilities such as cinemas, restaurants, and pubs. This complex sphere is administratively important as well, as two major sub-city offices are located here: Yeka and Bole. This area is well known as a center for transportation, having one of the major terminals in the city, from which it is possible to reach other major terminals in the city center and the eastern parts of the city. This area was recently designated as a subcenter of the city, and its significance as a focal point of the city is expected to increase (Addis Ababa City Planning Project Office [AACPPO] 2017: 52). With the city's expansion and the increase in traffic volume, Megenagna has become central in the eastern part of the city.

Public transport at Megenagna Terminal

Types of public transport

In the Megenagna Terminal, there are various types of public transportation that operate on 10 platforms. Figure 23 shows 10 platforms of public transportation with the division of five modes of transportation at the Megenagna terminal. There are five types of public transport services in operation. Three paratransit services operate: minibuses, *higer*, and *lonchon*. The other type is public buses, which are *anbessa* and *sheger* autobus. Each type of conveyance should work in a designated place, as shown in Figure. Table 9 shows the operating lines of each type of vehicle operating from a specific platform. In many cases, public buses and minibuses share the same routes, as is shown in the case of routes for Goro, Mexico, and Golagol. However, in some cases, only specific types of conveyances were designated to specific routes, such as *higer* and the *lonchon* were assigned for the long-distance route to K'aliti Terminal. Till the early 2000s, only platform-1 worked as a terminal. However, owing to the increase in traffic volume, the platform is divided into different sectors of the main street, which has shaped the current geographical features.

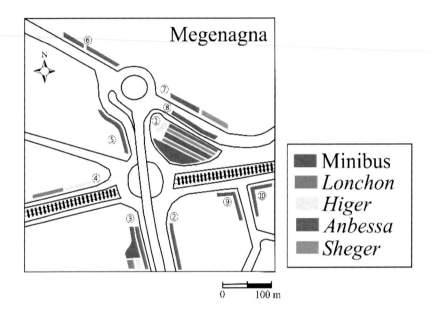

Figure 23. Place of operation by five modes of public transportations at Megenagna Terminal

Table 9. Operating routes by modes of public transportation at Megenagna Terminal

Platform number	Type of conveyances and operating destinations*
1	M: 5 (Kazanchis, Mexico, Semit, Meri, Merkato) L: 1 (K'aliti) H: 1 (K'aliti) A: 3 (Goro, Goro-2, Kolfe) S: 5 (Bole Arabsa, Semit, T'afo, Saris, D-49)
2	A: 3 (Tulu Dimtu, Koyefache Network, K'ilint'o)
3	M: 3 (Gerji, Gerji Mabrat Hail, Bole) A: 1 (Goro) L: 1 (Goro) H: 1 (Goro)
4	L: 2 (Mexico, Golagol) H: 2 (Mexico, Golagol)
5	M: 3 (Cinema Ethiopia - Piazza, Markato, Autobus Tera)
6	M: 3 (Sidist Kilo, Shiromeda, Piazza) A: 2 (Kara, Shiromeda)
7	A: 2 (Arat Kilo, Merkato) S: 2 (D-21, B-21)
8	M: 3 (Lega T'afo, Yeka Abado, Kotebe-Kara) A: 2 (Leta T'afo, Yeka Abado)
9	M: 1 (Semit)
10	M: 2 (Ayat, Ayat Ch'afe)

Source: Author's own observation from fieldwork in August 2019.
Note: Numbers are corresponding to those in the Figure 23.
* M: Minibus, L: *Lonchon*, H: *Higher* bus, A: *Anbessa* bus, S: *Sheger* bus

Minibus service

Among the public transportation systems that operate in the Megenagna terminal, minibuses are the most utilized mode of transport. In Megenagna, there were 22 minibus routes that connect the central, eastern, and southern parts of the city (Figure 24). Nine routes connected the center of the city that are heart of commerce, administration, and economy. Three routes connected Markato area (route 1-3) and Piazza (4), which is a center of commerce in Addis Ababa. It also connects Arat Kilo (5, 7), Sidist Kilo (6), and Mexico (8, 9), where many administrative offices commercial facilities are located. The southern part of Addis Ababa is connected by seven routes. It connects the newly emerged city center, Bole (10), and residential places such as Gerji (13), Gerji Mabrat Hail (14), and Goro (15). The minibus also operates long-distance destinations in the southern area (11, 12, and 16). Finally, six routes connect the eastern part of Addis Ababa (17—22). The eastern area was mostly a residential area that consists of condominium complexes, which have been built in 2003 under the state's urban management program.

In 2019, approximately 3,000 minibuses were designated to operate in this terminal. In Table 10, we can see that the number of vehicles that work in each route is different. The number of vehicles show huge gaps, from 17 (route-5) to 452 fleets (route-1). This amount is determined by the AARTB every month by considering the status of the road and transport demand. Thus, minibus operators should work in their designated route. However, each route has different profitability, and the preference of minibus operators also shows variances. Thus, many minibus workers often work in other terminals, which are called *berere* (በረረ, term which refers to minibuses operating in undesignated place). As these activities may cause traffic confusion, a supervisor from AARTB called *tek'ot'et'ari* (auditor) is dispatched to the terminal; however, this monitoring system is not well managed.

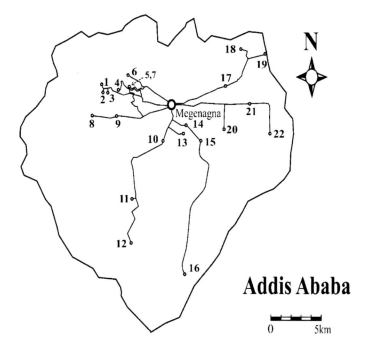

Figure 24. Map of minibus routes which departs from Megenagna Terminal

Table 10. Minibus routes at Megenagna Terminal

Route number	Destination	Length (km)	Tariff (*birr*)	Number of vehicles
1	Autobus Tera (አውቶቡስ ተራ)	9.4	6.0	452
2	T'ana Gebeya / Markato (ጣና ገበያ / መርካቶ)	8.2	6.0	167
3	Cinema Ras (ሲኒማ ራስ)	9.2	6.0	87
4	Piazza (ፒያሳ)	7.2	4.5	462
5	Arat Kilo (አራት ኪሎ)	5.0	3.0	17
6	Sidist Kilo (ስድስት ኪሎ)	5.0	3.0	123
7	Arat Kilo (አራት ኪሎ)	7.5	4.5	77
8	Tegbared (ተግባረዕድ)	6.5	4.5	104
9	Ethiopia Coffee and Tea Authority / Mexico (ቡናና ሻይ / ሜክሲኮ)	7.5	4.5	131
10	Bole Bras (ቦሌ ብራስ)	3.8	3.0	*n.d.*
11	Saris Abo (ሳሪስ አቦ)	11.5	7.5	181
12	Kaliti Total (ቃሊቲ ቶታል)	18.5	12.0	41
13	Gerji (ገርጂ)	3.4	3.0	*n.d.*
14	Gerji Mabrat Hail (ገርጂ መብራት ሃይል)	2.4	1.5	*n.d.*
15	Goro (ጎሮ)	5.0	3.0	34
16	Addis Ababa Science and Technology University (ከሳይንስና ቴክኖሎጂ ዩኒቨርሲቲ)	18.0	12.0	10
17	Kotebe - Kara (ኮተቤ - ካራ)	8.0	6.0	198
18	Yeka Abado (የካ አባዶ)	12.5	7.5	69
19	Lega T'afo - Mishen (ለገጣፎ - ሚሽን)	15.0	9.0	65
20	Semit (ሰሚት)	7.5	4.5	283
21	Ayat (አያት)	8.3	6.0	229
22	Ayat Ch'afe (አያት ጫፈ)	11.8	7.5	167
	Total			2,897

Source: Author's own observation in September 2019 with reference to AARTB (2019).
Note: Numbers are corresponding to those in the Figure 24.

Eight tera askebari groups

In Megenagna Terminal, the minibus management was operated by several *tera askebari* groups. Figure 25 presents the area of *tera askebari* groups recorded during fieldwork. The operating groups were A, B, C, D, E, F, Y, and Z. Including the groups whose operation forms were not revealed (referred to as *n.d.*), the number of *tera askebari* groups is expected to be 8 to 11 in this terminal.

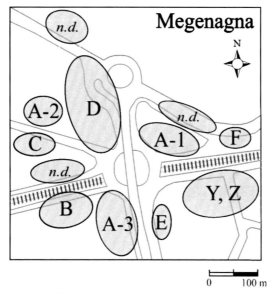

Figure 25. Map of *tera askebari* groups at Megenagna Terminal

Each group controlled and operated its business in a specific area, which is called *tera* among themselves.[16] Excluding the groups Y and Z, which share the same territory, intruding on the territories of other groups was forbidden. Through several trials and errors committed over decades, each group has strengthened its power in specific areas and solidified sovereignty in its respective *tera*. Thus, although these groups were working adjacent to each other, there was no significant connection between the groups. According to the interview of a manager of Group A (July 2018), he argued that seven *tera askebari* groups are operating and they do not interfere with the affairs of other groups. Some *tera askebari* in the researched area mentioned that they can neither intrude in others' *tera*, nor can they operate in their territories. For example, Mr. Amer, who are working in a Y, Z *tera* said, "That is not our *sefer* (appointing the E *tera*).[17] We cannot go there, and they also cannot work here" (Mr. Amer. 20s. *Tera askebari*. August 23, 2019). In this discourse, it is observed that the *tera* does not merely indicate a "workplace," but implying a kind of sense of belongings where individual *tera askebari* are belongs to.

Each group was organized by boss of the group called *wanna*. *Wanna* (ዋና)

means major or chief in Amharic. They were majorly consisted of the early *tera askebari*, who were developed from the street gangsters. When the government intervened to the early *tera askebari* in 2011, they registered to the MSEs program. When they register, they were required to fill in the place where they are going to operate the business. The registration process perpetuated the early *tera askebari*'s control and power over their territory. As per the information obtained so far, Group A, B, F, Y, and Z were registered for the MSEs program.

Group A comprised the largest group in this area. They were called as *wust lejoch* (ውስጥ ልጆች), which means "guys in the inner terminal" (Figure 26). According to the interview held with two *tera askebari* who worked in the A *tera*, they started their business in the early 2000s when the minibus business began in the area. As the *wanna* of group A was strong and influential, they could expand their territory up to A-2 and A-3. Currently, they have registered their groups for the MSEs program and handed over the practical management of the groups to the managers of each *tera*.

Figure 26. Photo of major platform at Megenagna Terminal (A-1 in the Figure 25)

Group B was called *haya arat lejoch* (ሀያ አራት ልጆች, means boys in the Haya Arat area). They received this name as the group was developed from the *haya arat* gangster group, which were influential in the Haya Arat area that is located under the B *tera*. Group C was run by strong leadership from the Wolaytta ethnic group. Wolaytta is a North Omotic language groups spoken in the southern part of Ethiopia. Unlike the other groups, the members of this group seemed to have strong ethnic identity and forming a high social relationship among each other. Not only the *tera askebari* business, but a majority of people who operate informal businesses at C *tera*, such as shoe shiner, street vendors, and *tera askebari*, originated from the Wolaytta ethnic groups. D *tera* was one of the lucrative platforms in this terminal, which bound to Arat Kilo and Piazza. The different characteristics between the groups show that their businesses have become highly pluralized and specialized, showing different operating forms and features, despite the fact that they working close to each other.

Groups Y and Z

Unlike most other *tera askebari* groups, in which one group supervises one specific area, my research site was run by two groups, which is Group Y and Group Z. Both groups were running by the leadership of *wanna*, who were registered in the MSEs program. From the late 1990s, the influential youths in this area were working at this terminal. When the MSEs development program was launched in 2011, around 10 members gathered and registered in the MSEs program under *woreda* Y, Bole Sub-city. However, forming a group and registering it for the MSEs program was only available to the residents of the same *woreda*. Thus, some *tera askebari*, who are not residents of *woreda* Y, could not join the process.

One day in 2017, some people argued their rights to operate the business at Platform X. They had a working experience with the members of Group Y, but were excluded in the registration process as they were not in the same *woreda* with them. They formed Group Z and registered it in the *woreda* Z. Following that, members of Group Z visited Platform X with the officers of MSEs agency and argued to start the business in the same terminal. Under the MSEs agency's regulation, each enterprise can operate its business in the *woreda* that it belongs to. Whereas Platform X was geographically located in the middle of the *woreda* Y and *woreda* Z, which led the Group Z to argue their rights. The officer in the *woreda* Z mentioned that two groups divided the work peacefully because both had a right to run their business. "The process was done peacefully. We went to the terminal together and discussed with the *tera askebari* of Group Y" (Officer of MSEs bureau at Woreda Z, 30s, male, Bole Sub City, October 28, 2019). Following that, two groups divided the weekly schedule, in which Group Y was working four days a week and the Group Z was working three days a week.

Group Y's management at Platform X

Research site: Southeastern part of Megenagna Terminal, Platform X

I conducted research at the southeastern part of the Megenagna terminal, which I refer to as Platform X. This terminal was predominantly used by minibuses, while *higer* buses and *lonchon* midi-buses seldom operated in the rush hours. The field site was spatially subdivided into two sections: the western and eastern sections (see Figure 4 in page 10). In the western section, two routes were in operation: Semit and Semit Condominium (Table 11). While Semit was a regular route allowed by the AARTB, Semit Condominium was the unpermitted route. In the eastern section, five routes were in operation. There were two permitted routes, Ayat and Ayat Chafe,[18] and three unpermitted routes, Gurd Shola, T'afo, and Bole Arabsa. The mixed operation of regular and irregular routes showed that the informal features of minibus businesses often run irregularly on the demand of the passengers and operators themselves. Based on the distance, passenger fares range from 1.5 to 10 *birr*.[19] The *tera askebari*'s service charge was called *sadi*, and it ranges from 5 to 20 *birr*.

To manage the minibuses, one group was in charge of two sections per day. Group Y was working four days a week and the Group Z was working three days a week. The two groups showed small disparities in relation to management, such as work schedule, form of subcontracting, and ability to manage the minibuses. Regardless of these differences, all the *tera askebari* in this terminal were generally responsible for three tasks: overseeing and maintaining the order of the minibuses, queuing of the passengers, and surveillance to check criminal activities such as robbery.

Table 11. Minibus routes, minibus fare and s*adi* at Platform X

Section	Route	Distance (km)	Permission from AARTB	Minibus fare	Sadi (service charge)
				*birr**	
Western	Semit	7.29	○	4.5	7
	Semit Condominium	9.76	✕	6.0	7
Eastern	Gurd Shola	1.93	✕	1.5	5
	Ayat	8.27	○	6.0	7
	Ayat Ch'afe	11.28	○	7.5	7
	T'afo	12.09	✕	7.5	7
	Bole Arabsa	14.71	✕	10.0	20

Source: Author's fieldwork.
* *Birr*: Ethiopian *birr* (1 USD = 29 Ethiopian *birr*, in September 2019)

Fare collecting system of Group Y

The early *tera askebari*, who initially formed Group Y and registered to the MSEs program, were acting as a boss, *wanna*, in the group. Meanwhile, at the research site, the work was conducted mostly by informally hired workers, that is Manager and YBs (Young Boys). *Wanna* hired two managers, Mgr-A and Mgr-B, to manage the general affairs in the terminal. Mgr-A controls the western section and Mgr-B controls the eastern section, and both hired two YBs under them.

Figure 27 shows the flowchart of money by Group Y *tera askebari* at Platform X. First, passengers paid the fare to the minibus operators (no. 1). Following that, the minibus operators were required to pay a service charge to *tera askebari*, specifically both managers and YBs, which was called as *sadi* (ሳዲ, a *tera askebari* service charge) among themselves (no. 2). Each of the managers in the two distinctive sections were managed separately. When the daily work finished around 18:30, the manager collected money from the employees. Following that, the managers leave the compulsory payments with the *wanna*, which is called *gebi* (ገቢ, literally means "income" but it refers to mandatory saving to *wanna*) (no. 3).[20] After that, they give the daily wage to their employees, which is called *jonata* (ጆናታ, slang which refers to a daily payment) (no. 4).[21]

While there were often differences in the amount collected, *tera askebari* usually collected service charges based on certain rules. Table 11 illustrates seven operating routes at this terminal: distance, permission status, passenger fare, and *sadi. Sadi* seems to vary depending on the amount of money a minibus driver can earn from passengers. For example, the shortest route at this terminal was Route-Gurd Shola, the passenger fare for which was 1.5 *birr*, and the *tera askebari* collected 5 *birr* as a service charge for one vehicle. In most of the cases, the *sadi* was 7 *birr* (Route-Semit, Semit Condominium, Ayat, Ayat Chafe, and T'afo), with passenger fares ranging from 4.5 to 7.5 *birr*. However, in the case of Route Bole Arabsa, the distance did not differ significantly from that of Route T'afo, but the *sadi* was 20 *birr*. This is because *tera askebari* collect *sadi* based on the amount of money each minibus can earn at once at the terminal, rather than the distance of the route. The AARTB did not permit minibuses to operate on Route Bole Arabsa, but it was always in high demand for passengers because there was a large condominium complex at its final destination. Therefore, despite

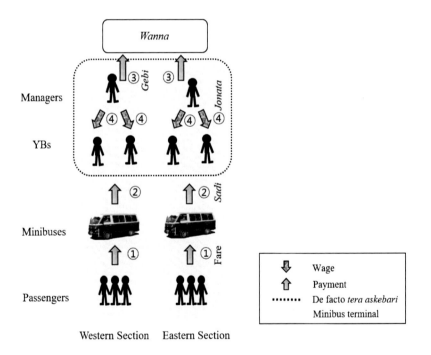

Figure 27. Group Y's fare collecting system

being illegal, many minibuses operated on the route, and the drivers did not hesitate to accept 20 passengers per vehicle, six more than what the regulations allowed. Since the minibuses that operate on Bole Arabsa have higher profit potential than the minibuses operating on other routes, a higher *sadi* was imposed.

Earning structure

In the case of Group Y, the profit of this terminal was approximately 10,000 *birr* per day. Table 12 presents the earnings of each section based on the calculations and interviews. The assumptive daily revenue from this terminal was around 10,000 *birr*, with 3,700 *birr* and 5,430 *birr* generated from the western and eastern sections, respectively. Different revenue amounts were generated from the number of routes that operate in each section.

Among this revenue, *wanna* requested 2,000 *birr* and 3,000 *birr* from managers in the western and eastern sections, which was more than half of the daily earnings. The revenue system of group Y was analyzed based on the observation of the daily expenditure of Mgr-A in the western section. For example, on October 17, 2019, Mgr-A had six expenditures. First, he had breakfast with YB-A and YB-B. While they were having the meal, Mgr-A hired two *fanta* (ፋንታ, slang which indicates substitute workers).[22] He paid 115 *birr* for breakfast and 25 *birr* for each *fanta*. They ate lunch individually, so substitute workers were not needed this time. Mgr-A gave YB-A and YB-B 50 *birr* each for lunch and spent 45 *birr* for his lunch. The work continued until 6:30 p.m. After work, Mgr-A paid YB-A and YB-B 200 *birr* each (*jonata*). However, the manager was not able to take all the money left as the day's work was over. He had to pay the compulsory payment, *gebi*, of 2,000 *birr*, which he should hand over to *wanna*. As the total earnings on that day was 3,160 *birr*, the manager was able to earn 450 *birr* at the time. However, compulsory payment was fixed at 2,000 *birr* per day.

This resulted in the creation of a reverse pyramid-type revenue structure: employees earn only 200 *birr* per person for around 12 hours' work, but the *wanna* earns more than half of the total earnings (70.2%) without providing any labor. The exact beneficiaries and distribution among the *wanna* should be further investigated, but the members of *wanna* had fixed daily income by only possessing the legal license that MSEs agency provided.

Table 12. Approximate daily earnings at Platform X

	Time	Time lapse	Western	Eastern
Morning shift	6:00~12:00	6h	1,100*	1,200*
Daytime	12:00~16:00	4h	800	1,000
	16:00~17:00	1h	1,000**	500***
Rush hour	17:00~18:30	1h30'		700
Night shift	18:30~21:00	2h30'	800	2,030****
Total revenue			3,700	5,430

Source: Majorly based on author's own calculation.
* Interview from YB. A in Sep 18 (wed), 2019.
** Observation: 15:50 to 18:30, total 2h 39' 41", in Sep 3 (Tue), 2019 Total earning: 7 *birr* x 145 = 1,015 *birr*.
*** Observation: 15:50 to 16:45, total 55' 02", in Sep 17 (Tue), 2019. Total earning: 7 *birr* x 72 = 504 *birr*.
**** Interview of YB-D in Sep 17 (Tue), 2019.

Government's transport policy and *wanna*'s continuance of power

The early *tera askebari* have quickly enrolled in the MSEs development program and received a formal license, which had a big merit for the early *tera askebari.* Under the MSEs development program, each *tera askebari* group was regarded as a private micro-enterprise. This means they could operate their business autonomously, without the government's intervention. In this condition, *tera askebari* develop their management methods independently, and this was the reason why the *wanna* of Group Y could create such an imbalanced earning structure. In other words, the *wanna* was utilizing the formality of the MSEs regulation and acting informally by subcontracting the daily workers and earning high benefits between these dynamics. Also, under the low government intervention, they were retaining their business rights up to the current moment.

Currently, the dominance of the early *tera askebari* continues, making it difficult for new young people to participate. The lucrative terminals had been already monopolized by the early *tera askebari* and their license has been prolonged. Also, the program's major aim, which was to develop the MSEs economic status, has discolored due to the government's low involvement and become major means of earning for the early *tera askebari*.

Then, why the government disregards the current *tera askebari* activity? Minibuses have been working as an indispensable means of transportation for citizens but were treated unfavorably by the government as they can easily cause traffic congestion. With the growing necessity of providing modern transportation services, the city government have been planning to construct BRT infrastructure, which aimed to increase the transport services led by the government (Banchialem 2017). Thus, with the future importance declining, investing in the minibus business is not a good option for the government in the long term. In this situation, the government transferred responsibility to *tera askebari* by maintaining the current minibus management system instead of actively intervening in it. With the MSEs program allowing *tera askebari* to operate autonomously, the government did not interfere in the way they operate the business. In other words, the government's passive attitude to develop the paratransit industry and the characteristics of the MSEs program created a background of *wanna*'s behavioral patterns and enabled them to maintain their power until the current moment and maximize their profits by acting informally.

Summary

This chapter aimed to observe the influence of the MSE program on the current business management of the *tera askebari*. Since 1990s, the MSEs received attention as a source of economic growth in developing countries. In Addis Ababa, about 40% of the urban labor force are engaged in the MSEs activities, which led the city administration to establish MSEs development program in 2011. Its major objective was to develop MSEs as a way to reduce poverty and solve unemployment, which can further accelerate economic growth of the state.

Before the MSEs program, there were several attempts from government side to intervene on *tera askebari*'s activities. However, it did not made success as the employment condition that it provides was not satisfied to the *tera askebari*. Unlike previous attempts that have failed to involve the *tera askebari*'s participation, the government has achieved success in drawing *tera askebari* through the MSEs development project. It was because first, the work was regarded as "their own business," which led the *tera askebari*'s involvement much easier. Second, there were high enforcement to formalize the informal business in the street, which have led the large-scale involvement of *tera askebari* to MSEs program.

In the early days, the *woreda* offices proposed *tera askebari* to operate with certain rules. However, these suggestions were not well maintained. First, the ticketing service with 1.25 *birr* did not last long, as it was inconvenient for *tera askebari* to issue a ticket and manage the minibus simultaneously. Second, most *tera askebari* were still maintaining their business even after the pledged period. Lastly, their saving practice raised a question on the MSEs program. As for the one group, their daily earning was around 6,000 to 8,000 *birr* per day, but their daily saving varied from 800 to 6,000 *birr*. It was because *tera askebari* does not find merits to save their assets in the MSEs program, and furthermore, there were high distrust among *tera askebari* on the transparency of the program. Thus, the uncertainty of the future promise and the weak involvement, the *tera askebari* were not passionate to increase their assets.

The Group Y's case in Platform X in Megenagna terminal was observed to understand the *tera askebari*'s activities after the government intervention. The *tera askebari* possesses the legal license were called *wanna*, and were leaders of the group. They hired workers to substitute their work, without providing any labor. The employees and manager were collecting the money from each minibus, but they need to pay most of their earnings to *wanna*. After that, their daily wages were divided among the remaining. Among the total revenue, more than half of the daily earnings were obliged to send to the *wanna*, while none of them were practically managing the minibuses in the terminal.

Currently, the dominance of the early *tera askebari* continues, making it difficult for new people to participate in creating a new *tera askebari* business. On the bottom of this phenomenon meanwhile, there is a government intention on the paratransit policy. The government aimed to construct BRT infrastructure while decreasing the numbers of minibuses due to environmental, political, and social problems. While the importance of minibus is decreasing, the government does not actively intervene to the *tera askebari* issue but transfer the management as well as the responsibility to *tera askebari*. Along with the MSEs program which allows *tera askebari* to operate autonomously, the early *tera askebari* were able to maintain their power until the current moment, as well as create an imbalanced earning structure, which maximize their benefits, while the current management is done by the young boys, who are live for a daily survival.

Notes

[1] To figure out determinants of MSEs development, see Markos et al. (2015) and Yared (2018). See Gemechu & Reilly (2011) on the analysis of effectiveness of policies.

[2] Ethiopia uses its own calendar system, which is seven years behind the Gregorian calendar. Also, the new year starts at September 11. In this regard, it is often to write Gregorian year like 2004/05 to refer 1996 fiscal year in Ethiopian calendar.

[3] *Woreda* is a smallest administrative unit in Ethiopia.

[4] It is called *sra fet'ere* (ስራ ፈጠረ) in Amharic.

[5] 1 USD was equivalent to 16.9 Ethiopian *birr* in the time of 2011. Searched at <https://www.ceicdata.com/en/ethiopia/exchange-rates-and-real-effective-exch ange-rates/et-official-exchange-rate-average-per-usd>

[6] 1 USD was equivalent to 8.6 Ethiopian *birr* in the time of 2005. Searched at <https://exchangerates.org/usd/etb/in-2005>

[7] The security guards who monitor the illegal operations taking place on the streets were called as *denb tera askebari* (ደንብ ተራ አስከባሪ), which means a rule keeper in Amharic.

[8] 1 USD was equivalent to 16.9 Ethiopian *birr* in the time of 2011. Searched at <https://www.ceicdata.com/en/ethiopia/exchange-rates-and-real-effective-exc hange-rates/et-official-exchange-rate-average-per-usd>

[9] Interview from one *tera askebari* at Bole Bras, July 5, 2017.

[10] Interview from one *tera askebari* at Semit, July 8, 2017.

[11] He mentioned "ይደብራል (*yidebral*)," meaning not only boring but also annoying and troublesome.

[12] See page 236, 659, and 678 of Leslau (1973).

[13] The major center in eastern part of Addis Ababa in 1960s was Shola Market (ሾላ ገበያ), which located about 600 meters western part of the Megenagna, that currently working as second-largest market in the city.

[14] 1 USD was equivalent to 2.5 Ethiopian *birr* in the time of 1960s. 1 *santim* are equivalent to 0.01 *birr*. Searched at <https://www.ceicdata.com/en/ethiopia/ exchange-rates-and-real-effective-exchange-rates/et-official-exchange-rate-averag e-per-usd>

[15] The construction of the Ring Road has geographically formed the Megenagna with diverse features, which has upper roads, lower roads, and railways. This also influenced the minibus operators to operate in different parts

at Megenagna. The place where upper roads were located were called *lay sefer* and the lower roads were called *tach sefer* among the *tera askebari*. *Lay sefer* was also called as "diaspora" naming to the Diaspora Apartment located near.

[16] *Tera* does not only mean queue, but it also refers to a specific area as well. For example, an area that sells Ethiopian coffee pots in Markato is called *jebena tera* (ጀበና ተራ, coffee pot area) and area that sells the vehicle glass is called *mascot tera* (መስኮት ተራ, window area).

[17] According to the interview of a manager of Group A (July 2018), he argued that seven *tera askebari* groups are operating and they do not interfere with the affairs of other groups.

[18] Ayat Chafe was also called as Arba Zet'egn in the field site. The name Arba Zet'egn (አርባ ዘጠኝ, literally means 49 in Amharic) has received its name as the *anbessa* bus that operates via Ayat Chafe Condominium with the number 49.

[19] 1 USD was equivalent to 29 Ethiopian *birr*, in September 2019. Searched at < https://www.exchangerates.org.uk/USD-ETB-spot-exchange-rates-history-2019 .html >

[20] *Gebi* is called as *gideta* (ግዴታ, obligation) as well.

[21] *Jonata* is also called as *jonta* (ጆንታ, slang which refers to a daily payment) or *yek'anu kefeya* (የቀኑ ከፍያ, daily payment).

[22] *Fanta* was also called *amarache* (አማራጭ), which means alternative.

Chapter 5. YBs' Livelihood and Dynamics of Coping Strategy

Introduction

Employment insecurity in the African transport industry

The African informal economy is a major source of employment, and approximately 85.8% of the total employment are working in the informal economy (ILO 2018: 13—14). The informal economy accounts for about 50% the gross domestic product (GDP) in Sub-Saharan Africa (AfDB 2013; Medina et al. 2017: 13). While the formal wage sector is not expected to create enough jobs in proportion to the rapidly growing population, the size of Africa's informal economy and the number of its informal workers are expected to increase further (Guven & Karlen 2020).

Despite the informal sectors' important role in the functioning of the African economy, the growth of this sector has raised several questions regarding employment insecurity. This has been a major issue in the African transport sector as well. The public transport industry has been creating vast employment opportunities for the youth owing to its relatively low entry barriers compared to specialized jobs (Berhanu 2017: 102). Furthermore, this sector has been a major income source for rural migrants and those who could not benefit from the modern education system (Richard & Happy 2008: 219; Gibbs 2014). However, most of informal workers face insecure working conditions, as this sector provides low-income security and low social protection (AfDB 2013). For example, most minibus attendants in Addis Ababa are making verbal agreement with the drivers. Furthermore, 83% of the *dala dala* motorbike taxi workers in Tanzania were working without entering into any contract (see Rizzo 2011: 1185).

Two major causes of transport workers' employment instability have been addressed. The first is the existence of a "structure" that exploits daily laborers. Here, the term "structure" implies the groups or industries that hold "power" (e.g., trade unions, owners, associations, and associated politics). Along with urbanization, the African transport sector has evolved into a big industry that has been attracting a considerable amount of monetary investment since the mid-1980s (Kenda 2006: 554). As the business grew, those who held power, either owners or supervisors, formed cartels to strengthen their vested interests

(Lee-Smith 1989: 287). These groups often conspired with the state by lobbying for sizeable benefits (Rizzo 2011: 1201). While the dominating structural power strengthened their interests, the labor conditions of the employed gradually weakened; this made the industry exploitative for workers, and their contracts still remained informal and precarious which subjected the workers to insecure working relations (Doherty 2017; Siyabulela 2021: 141-142).

The other explanation for the transport labor situation is the over-supply of labor. Due to increasing rural migration and urban development, most African cities are now experiencing rapid population growth. In particular, in a situation where the formal labor market cannot provide enough jobs for the youth, many unemployed youths are finding their way into the informal market. Because of the overflowing workforce in the labor market, the power balance is tilting, reducing their wages. For these reasons, transport workers in Africa are facing insecure working conditions and challenges with regard to the labor market. For example, the over-supply of *dala dala* workers' services in the labor market caused them to fail in their attempts to negotiate with the powerful bus owners, compelling them to undertake transgressive activities (Rizzo 2017: 71-76).

Discourse of precariousness and vulnerability of African transport workers

For a long time, major analyses of the informal economy have regarded informal workers as marginalized and passive beings, who lack the will and ability to advance into the formal sector. This analysis was based on dichotomous perspectives that regard formal and informal as "superior" and "inferior," respectively. Many policymakers and scholars depict informal workers as the most vulnerable, disadvantaged, and unprotected groups or individuals (Trebilcock 2005: 19-20). Often, their activities are regarded as being necessity-driven, and they are considered to be pushed into the realm by their "inability to find employment" in the formal economy.

Through the development of the study, it is understood that the dichotomous view in regarding formal and informal as being "good" and "bad" are not efficient for understanding the complex phenomena that occur in the current society. This increased the importance of observing the practices of those in the informal sector, such as how they communicate and interact, how they strategize, and how they negotiate with the formal sector. The informal workers choose different methods for maintaining their livelihoods (see Rakodi & Lloyd-Jones 2002; Lindell 2010: 25-26) and able to articulate their own voices (Bayat 2004: 94-97; Meagher 2010).

Despite continuous efforts to break the dualistic perspectives, the transport workers in Africa are still portrayed negatively. Those who hold power in the industry (e.g., marshals, owners, and associations) are portrayed as progressive beings, making their voices heard and having their demands fulfilled (Kenda 2017: 159). Meanwhile, workers on the ground, such as minibus attendants who works with the driver and touts who touts passengers at the terminal, are largely portrayed as being weak and vulnerable. They are also regarded as precarious and vulnerable, being easily impacted by the state forces and the exploitative system (Rizzo 2011: 1200). Various modifiers have been used to describe them, such as "young men in impossible positions" (Mbugua 2013: 212), or "precariat"[1] (Siyabulela 2021: 145), or "disposable people" (Doherty 2017).

This bisected tendency, which is divided into the powerful and the powerless, has weakened the voice of the informal workers, or excluded impliedly, and constructed them as precarious beings. However, their voices are existing undoubtedly, and they are trying to make better choices. They are adopting different strategies, such as transferring to other jobs, exploiting diverse work opportunities, and improving mobility and earnings (Tom 2015). They also are making collective efforts toward organization and struggle to achieve their rights (Rizzo & Atzeni 2020). For example, callboys in Malawi adopted several strategies when they faced a state ban on touting practices (Richard & Happy 2008).

Objective and research question

Based on the study observations of urban migrant youths' everyday job-seeking activities at minibus terminals, this chapter argues that African transport workers are subjective entities who have the power to decide and high adaptability to cope with an unstable environment. The subjects of the research were young boys (YBs) who migrated from a rural area and found work opportunities at Platform X. The main aim of this study is to examine the occupation choice strategies of YBs among several types of transport-related work. This chapter formulated three research questions. First, what does the "Terminal Community" mean to YBs? Second, what is the reason for their choice of occupation? Third, what are their strategies for coping with the unstable labor market? Thus, this chapter presents new ethnography of youths in the African transport sector, and it attempts to investigate their subjectivity by observing their personal livelihood strategies and examining their occupational mobility.

At Platform X, 29 transport workers were found to be affiliated with the

Terminal Community. Four of them were *wanna* (ዋና, leaders or boss of the group), and two are managers. There were 26 YBs (young boys) and they could be regular or part-time *tera askebari*; they were hired by the *wanna* and the managers without specified terms and labor contracts. While some YBs worked regularly as *tera askebari*, there were others who changed their occupation frequently. This fact inspired me to enquire whether it was proper to term the YBs as "*tera askebari*" when they lost their occupation. Thus, I aimed to use the term "YBs" to explain the trajectory of their occupations more efficiently.

In this chapter, I first explain the process by which rural immigrants become part of the Terminal Community. Second, I introduce two kinds of working strategies adopted by YBs in the *tera askebari* occupation. After that, I explain YBs' diversification strategies with regard to other types of transport works. Lastly, I explain how the Terminal Community works as a platform for YBs to develop to the next stage of life.

Livelihood of Young Boys (YBs) at Platform X

YBs at Platform X

The term "YBs" refers to male youths affiliated with the Terminal Community at Platform X. There were 23 YBs and all of them were male. Their age groups were comprised from teenagers to 30s. Those in their 20s formed the majority of the Terminal Community (61%, n=14), followed by those in their 30s (30%, n=7), and two teenagers (9%, n=2). The majority of this community consisted of rural immigrants who came to the city to find better employment opportunities (95.6%, n=22). The YB group's ethnic makeup included 4 major ethnic groups: Hadiya, Wolaytta, Oromo, and Gurage. Most of the YBs were from the Hadiya community (65%, n=15), followed by the Wolaytta (13%, n=3), the Oromo (9%, n=2), and the Gurage (4%, n=1). When we compare the major ethnic groups in Addis Ababa are Amhara (47%), Oromo (19.5%), Gurage (16.3%), and Tigrayan (6.18%) (CSA 2007), the demographic of Terminal Community shows distinctive features that is consisted with minor community, especially those from southwestern part of Ethiopia (n=19, 82%).

Background of YBs joining the Terminal Community

The YBs at Platform X were inducted by former YBs through their activities called *mek'erareb* (መቀራረብ), which means "to drag near" in Amharic. Thus, former YBs who were affiliated with the community invited their acquaintances into the community and introduced them to the community members as well as the *wanna* and managers. "At first, I started working because of my friend's suggestion" (interview from YB-A). YB-A told me that he was introduced by a YB who was working under Group Z. He was directly introduced to the *wanna* and was able to start working as a *tera askebari*. As in his case, some of the YBs started working directly after being introduced to the *wanna* or managers. However, in many other cases, YBs obtained job opportunities after being introduced into the community. "I know YB-K, and he introduced me to Mgr-B around one and a half years ago" (interview from YB-J). YB-J was acquainted with YB-K as he was living in the same village. YB-K saw that YB-J had no job, so he introduced him to the Terminal Community. When he joined the group, he could not start working directly as there was no vacancy, but after a while, when a position opened, he was able to start working.

Relationship between mek'erareb and the Hadiya-majority community

Most of the YBs in this terminal were rural immigrants, primarily from the Hadiya ethnicity. This raises the question as to why Hadiya dominates the worker population of this terminal. The orthodox view of the informal economy has regarded ethnicity as an important factor for urban migrators because it helps them form mutual relationships to ensure better survival and preparation for any future shocks (see Andreasen 1990; Lesetedi 2003). However, YBs did not seem to have a single strong ethnicity, nor did they have strong relations among themselves; rather, based on my observation, they were not willing to help each other when they faced problems. To me, it seemed that they were closer to the solitary hyenas that try to survive individually, rather than social animals that form groups and live together.

The answer for why the Hadiya ethnicity forms the majority was based on the areas in which they live. Most of them lived in a place called Gurd Shola.[2] Gurd Shola is located in *Woreda* 7, Bole Sub-city, which is only 2 km east of Platform X. It is a residential and commercial area where many immigrants have settled down because of low house rents. In 2012, a politician called Hailemariam Desalegn, who was of Wolaytta ethnicity and hailed from the southern part of Ethiopia, was designated as the prime minister of the country. As persons from southern ethnic groups rarely became country heads, many youths from the south migrated to the city, expecting that they would benefit from this political arrangement. Many of them settled down in cheap shantytowns and Gurd Shola was one of their choices. In this community, most of the YBs were living in Gurd

Shola (n=20, 87%), which is majorly inhabited by immigrants. Thus, the former YBs induct new YBs to the community, which were based on the networks in the Gurd Shola. This formed the current feature of the immigrant-majority community, which mostly consisted of Hadiya.

Economic status of YBs

Residential area

Housing is a physical symbol of people's living standards. By observing the YBs' residential type, we can obtain a sketchy image of their standard of living and individual economic levels. Most of the YBs resided in a place called Gurd Shola. Specifically, they were living in an area called *ch'erek'e sefer* (ጨረቃ ሰፈር, moon village). *Ch'erek'e* means "moon" and *sefer* means "the village" in Amharic. This name is derived from the compound noun, *ch'erek'e bet* (ጨረቃ ቤት), which literally means "moon house." *Ch'erek'e bet* is an informal type of housing that is constructed overnight when the moon has risen; this construction process is designed to escape government control and surveillance (Eliyas 2018: 24). It is mostly a survival type of housing in that it is informal and generally occupied by rural migrants. The construction type includes mostly *chek'a bet* (ጭቃ ቤት, mud house), a house with walls made of wood and mud, and roofs covered with *k'orek'oro* (ቆርቆሮ, corrugated iron). The *ch'erek'e sefer* in Gurd Shola received its name because of the abundance of *ch'erek'e bet* and other types of informal housing.

The *ch'erek'e sefer* in Gurd Shola was largely inhabited by migrants from rural areas. According to the interviews, the major ethnic groups residing in this area were the Hadiya, the Wolaytta, the Oromo, and a small number of Tigray people. In the early 2000s, the area was almost empty with few residents. Since the mid-2000s, the number of residents in this area has been increasing, and in 2021, it has become one of the most populous areas in Addis Ababa. Figure 28 shows an aerial view taken through Google Earth (Image date: April 29, 2021) (longitude 38.8243~38.8324, latitude 9.0078~9.0176, 823,314 m2). The red circled line is an area of the *ch'erek'e sefer* in Gurd Shola. In 2001, the area had few residents and houses. In 2003, people started inhabiting the area, and half of it became occupied. The number of residents was continually increasing, and in 2021, it was difficult to find an empty habitation in this area. The officer of *woreda* 7, who was in charge of this area, illustrated that the registered population of Gurd Shola was 46,000 in 2019; however, this officer expected the number of residents in the area to double if informal housings are included.[3]

Figure 28. Aerial view of Gurd Shola from 2001 to 2021 (*Source*: Google Earth)

Residence type

Most YBs were living in poor environments. Table 13 shows the residence types of the four YBs in the time of research period. All of them were living in a one-room house. They used a common lavatory that they shared with multiple households, and the sanitation facilities were inadequate. In the case of YB-N, a shower system was installed in the lavatory. However, the condition of this construction was weak in that the showerhead was installed right above the toilet; thus, the water used flowed directly into the toilet below. Others used common tap water for washing or public shower rooms in the village, which cost 7 to 15 *birr* per use. A cold-water shower cost 7 *birr*, while a hot water shower cost 15 *birr*. Except for YB-B, who earned and helped his family in his hometown, other YBs were living with multiple community members. YB-A and YB-N were living with his family, while YB-S shared one room with his friends.

All of them were living in a confined space, which seems not sufficient for the multiple people. Figure 29 shows the house plan for YB-A's house. Besides himself, this residence was inhabited by four family members. Five households in the compound were using one lavatory, which was located next to YB-A's house. The house's front yard was commonly used for hanging out the laundry, drying the *injera* (እንጀራ, Ethiopian flat bread that is made with a grain called *teff*), or washing the dishes. The dimension of this accommodation was around 6.62 square meters, which excluded the common lavatory. Because the space of beds was insufficient for four family members, two members spread blankets on the floor to sleep on. The living space for one person was only 1.65 square meters. This numerical value shows a low living standard, which is far below the living standards of other countries. In the case of Japan, the minimum housing standard for one person is 16 square meters (Kim & Yoon 2009: 49), and in the case of South Korea, it is 14 square meters (Choi & Jeong 2011: 119). However, in the case of YB-A, four members were living in an area of 6.62 square meters, which was half the size of one person's minimum housing standard in Japan and South Korea.

YBs' rental ranged from 1,300 to 1,500 *birr* per month (equivalent to 44.8 to 51.7 USD [1 USD=29 *birr*, during the period of September 2019]). This amount is comparatively cheaper than that for other areas of similar size in Addis Ababa. For comparison, during the fieldwork, I was living in a room that was similar in size to that of YB-N (about 1.9m x 4.3m=8.17 square meters). It had a lavatory together with a showerhead, which was installed above the toilet. However, it was located in the center of the city, and the rental fee was about double that paid by YB-N (3,300 *birr*=113.8 USD).

Table 13. Residence type of four YBs

ID	Residence type	Lavatory	Shower	Living type	Rental fee (*birr*)
YB-A	One-room	Communal	X	4 people (Mother, brother, sister & YB-A)	1,300
YB-B	One-room	Communal	X	YB-B	1,500
YB-N	One-room	Communal	O	4 people (Wife, two children & YB-N)	1,500
YB-S	One-room	Communal	X	3 people (two friends & YB-S)	1,200

Source: Author's fieldwork.

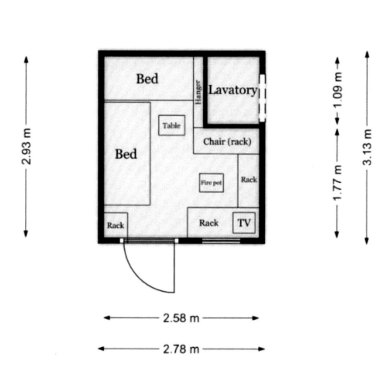

Figure 29. House plan of YB-A's house

Living condition of YB-A

YB-A had a wide forehead, big eyes, and was a 25-year-old young man. He was born in 1994 (1987 in the Ethiopian calendar) in a small town near Hosaena city. His mother was from the Hadiya community, and his father was from the Gurage community. His family was actively engaged in farming, but this livelihood did not earn them a sufficient amount of money. His family decided to move back to Addis Ababa when he was 14. YB-A's family settled in Gurd Shola, where many rural migrants had settled. They found a house in *the ch'erek'e sefer*, where many rural migrants had settled for low rentals. The monthly rent was 800 *birr*. His mother went out to work in a restaurant, but she earned only about 1,000 *birr* per month. YB-A's father did not support them financially. Although his step-sibling's father sometimes sent them money (about 1,000 *birr*), this amount was insufficient for their sustenance. Since then, YB-A was responsible for making a living. To support his family, especially his younger siblings' school education, he started working as a shoe-shiner and minibus attendant. He says he was forced to do everything to put food on the table, eat one better meal, and pay rent. When he was 22 years old, his friend asked him whether he would be willing to work as a *tera askebari*, and from that moment onward, he began to work as a *tera askebari*.

During my fieldwork, I found that all his family members (mother, younger brother, and younger sister) relied on his income for sustenance. His mother could not sustain the work due to her poor health condition. His brother had already dropped out of high school in his first year and was not doing any productive work. His sister was attending middle school, and YB-A supported her to buy some educational materials. He also paid the house rent, which amounted to 1,300 *birr* per month. His income ranged from 2,600 *birr* to 4,040 *birr* (89.6 USD to 139.3 USD) between November and February. After paying the house rent, he was left with a total of 1,400 *birr* and 2,840 *birr* (48.3 USD to 97.9 USD), which was lower than the minimum monthly living wage for single typical family in Addis Ababa, 5,940 *birr* (see WageIndicator.org 2022).

Individual background of tera askebari in other terminals

For many youths, the *tera askebari* work was a means of making a living. Several *tera askebari* across different terminals stated that they had no other choice but to work as *tera askebari*. One sweltering hot day, Mr. Bre and I sat in a burger shop near the Piazza minibus station, ordered a cup of tea, and started a conversation. He had an exotic appearance with a high nose and sharp features, which was different from the other Ethiopians. After hearing his personal history, I realized that my guess was not wrong.

Mr. Bre said:

> "*My mother was beautiful, but she had no money. She worked at a bar, met an Italian man, and gave birth to me. I heard my father was a businessman. But I never saw him, and I did not know what exactly he worked.... My mother and I ate bula (leftover food from a restaurant or hotel) and lived day after day.... I was young and poor. I was simply an abandoned street boy. Therefore, I started to work with the tera askebari. At that time, the work was easy. I touted the destination with a loud voice and received a few pennies from the driver*" (Mr. Bre. 40s. Tera askebari. July 10, 2018, Piazza Arada).

Mr. Bre told me about his unhappy childhood. His mother gave birth to him against her will, as she had only a short-term relationship with an Italian guest. His family could not afford any food, so he had to go out into the street and do all kinds of work, including selling chewing gums, polishing shoes, and working as a minibus attendant, to make a pittance. He had also joined the *tera askebari* to make his living. According to him, it was a poverty that made him to come out to the street and start *tera askebari*.

On the other hand, many *tera askebari* said that they started *tera askebari* work because there were no other jobs available. Mr. Mamo, who argued that he was educated, said that he had started *tera askebari* work because of the lack of jobs.

He said:

> "*I graduated after I reached the 12th grade. My grandfather fought in the Korean War. Many of our team members were educated and smart. But there was no work! Society made us do this job. I am just sitting here the whole day, and I earn 400 birr a month*" (Mr. Mamo. 40s. Tera askebari. July 20, 2018, Arat Kilo Terminal).

Mr. Mamo had a special family history; his grandfather was a veteran of the Korean War. He said he was educated, stating that he had graduated in the 12th grade. However, despite his diploma, he could not find proper work; this situation led him to start the *tera askebari* work. He had been often visited the terminal to spend some time with his friend, and this led him to work as a *tera askebari*.

Seeking the chance to work as *tera askebari*

For the YBs, the Terminal Community functioned as a platform that provided them various working opportunities. Platform X was a space for socialization, where YBs established interpersonal networks and broadened opportunities by interacting with the *tera askebari* cadre (*wanna* and manager) as well as the minibus operators.

Working in a regular position

The first work opportunities which YBs can get was *tera askebari*. The work of *tera askebari* was divided into two types. The first was a regular position, and the other was a part-time position. The regular position refers to work opportunities in which YBs make contracts with the managers or *wanna* to work on a designated time and schedule, whereas the part-time position involved instant contract work whereby the YBs worked on an ad-hoc basis.

The first work chance was in a regular position. In this terminal, two groups were working on different days (Figure 30). Group Y's work was divided into the day shift (6:00 to 18:30) and the night shift (18:30 to 20:00). Under the leadership of the *wanna*, two managers managed the four YBs: YB-A, B, C, and D. These four YBs worked in a regular position, in which the work lasted from around 6:00 to 18:30. The night shift, which was run on an ad-hoc basis, started after 18:30. Their daily wages were 200 *birr* for working approximately 12 hours. On the other hand, Group Z's working schedule was divided into three terms: shift-1 (6:00 to 12:00), shift-2 (12:00 to 15:00), and shift-3 (15:00 to 20:00). *Wanna* in Group Z preferred to hire YBs directly, so there was no manager who controls them. Six YBs worked in a regular position, that is, YB-A, E, L, M, F, and G. These YBs earned 100 to 150 *birr* when they worked on one shift. In both groups, the wages showed little variance depending on the working experience.

Their working conditions were poor in that they had to run whole day and work regardless of the weather. Their working environment was also poor, and the working site was hazardous of hundreds of vehicles moving a day. In particular, during the rainy season, they did not have a single roof to protect them. At noon, the weather became extremely hot that the heat of the asphalt could melt the soles of their shoes. One *tera askebari* mentioned about the working condition,

"The work is really difficult. We are often insulted by the *woreda* officer, police, and assistants. Especially, due to the severe air pollution, I feel that my health is worsening every day. It is not an easy job" (Mr. Mikael. 40s. July 12, 2018, Kara Terminal).

However, the high amounts of daily wages they can get compared to other types of informal works has become merit for them to choose this position. Table 14 shows the wages of informal workers and the wages of the *tera askebari* who were working in Addis Ababa. The guard's and janitor's monthly wages were 800 and 1,000 *birr*, respectively. When we divide this amount by 30 days, their daily wage was 26.6 to 33.3 *birr*. The shoe shiner earned approximately 50 *birr* (net profit) per day at my research site. However, the *tera askebari*'s daily wages, whether those of Group Y or Group Z, showed that they could earn a higher daily wage than the other types of informal workers.

Also, there were some chances to hide their earnings in the pocket. YBs collect service charges directly from the minibus attendants and then hand over the whole earnings to managers of *wanna* when their shifts are over. Thus, some YBs hid some of their earnings. As an example, YB-A's daily earning in Group Y was 200 *birr*, while he often earned more than 300 *birr* a day due to the concealed cash. This may be one of the merits for the YBs to stick into the *tera askebari* work despite the unfair earning structure.

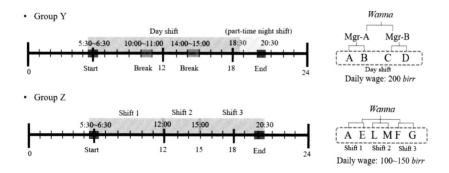

Figure 30. Timetable and organizational structure of Group Y and Group Z

Table 14. Wage of informal workers in Addis Ababa

Occupation	Monthly wage	Daily wage*
Guard	800	26.6
Janitor	1,000	33.3
Shoe shiner	1,400	50
Regular position, Group Y	3,200 (4 days a week)	200
Regular position, Group Z	1,300~1,950 (3 days a week)	100~150

Source: Author's fieldwork, estimate monthly and daily wage based on interview.
* Daily wage is calculated as monthly wage / 30.

Seeking the work opportunities

Regular position

Although the regular position provided high wages, not everyone could get the opportunities. While there were 23 YBs in this terminal, only 10 positions were open for them (4 in Group Y and 6 in Group Z). Furthermore, the number of people who could work in one shift was limited to two to four. Thus, there was high competition among the YBs with regard to taking regular work opportunities. Under these conditions, what strategies do unemployed YBs choose? The first strategy was to keeping the connection with the Terminal Community and interacting with the managers and *wanna*. Through this, workers could get a "chance" to receive regular or part-time position.

Figure 31 shows the working period associated with YBs' regular position in group Y from August 2018 to February 2020. During fieldwork (August to October 2019), YB-A and YB-B were working under Mgr-A, and YB-C and YB-D were working under Mgr-B. In this figure, the observable point is the irregular working period. YBs' working period was irregular in that it differed between 19 days (YB-U), 1 month (YB-*n.d.*), and 1 year and a half (YB-A and YB-C). Some YBs left the work voluntarily (YB-B and YB-U), while others were dismissed by their managers due to personal conflicts (YB-A, YB-C, and YB-D). This irregularity of working period implies that the availability of regular working opportunities was unpredictable.

When the YBs left the job, it was found that other YBs who often visited the terminal were able to fill in their vacancies. YB-U, YB-J, YB-C, and YB-M, who took regular positions after YB-A, YB-B, YB-*n.d.*, and YB-D had left, all had earlier frequently visited the terminal, formed a good relationship with the *tera askebari* cadre, and also occasionally worked as part-time *tera askebari.* YB-U had worked during the breakfast break under Mgr-A. YB-J and YB-M also had experience working as part-time workers. In the case of YB-C, although he was dismissed by Mgr-B because of an argument, he was able to resume work after apologizing to Mgr-B. These examples show that the YBs who had connections with the *tera askebari* cadre had a higher probability of being selected as regular *tera askebari* than those who did not have any such connections.

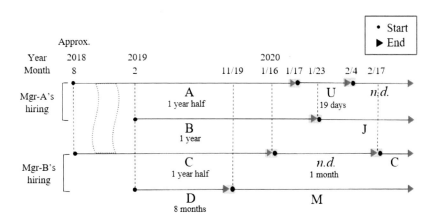

Figure 31. Working period of regular position in Group Y

Part-time position

By visiting the terminal, YBs could also be able to get part-time jobs. There were three types of part-time positions. The first is working during a *tera askebari*'s mealtime. When the *tera askebari* went to take their meal breaks, YBs who stayed at the terminal could get the opportunity. This work time lasted approximately 1 hour, and the wages ranged from 25 to 30 *birr*. For example, YB-U worked temporarily from 10 to 11 a.m. when the *tera askebari* in the western section went for breakfast. He earned 25 *birr* per hour. The second involved working at nighttime. In the case of Group Y, the night shift done from 18:30 to around 20:30 to 21:30 (end of the minibus service). By working for two to three hours, YBs could receive 70 to 120 *birr*. Unlike the regular position, the managers hire YBs who stays in the terminal on ad hoc basis. The third type was to work in the regular workers' vacancies. Due to personal circumstances, there were some days when YBs in regular positions were unable to work. For example, YB-A traveled to his hometown during the public holiday of *meskel* (መስቀል)[4] (September 26 to 29, 2019). During this period, YB-K worked on YB-A's vacancies.

YB-L's strategy to get a part-time opportunity

In the time of fieldwork, YB-L was working at shift-1 (6:00 to 12:00) in Group Z. On the morning of September 23, YB-L asked YB-E to give him the money that he earned during the shift so that he could take it directly to *wanna*. YB-E questioned YB-L as to whether he had embezzled money during the course of his work. This enraged YB-L, causing a severe quarrel and physical altercation between them. *Wanna*-A, who heard about the incident, suggested that YB-L should take a break and laid off. After the dismissal from the work, however, YB-L experienced economic difficulties.

In this situation, he went to Platform X to find work opportunities. On November 19, 2019, YB-L set out to seek job opportunities around 15:00 but could not find work opportunities (see Table 15). On November 20, YB-L found that YB-G was absent from his shift at 12:00. He called *Wanna*-A and asked for permission to work in the absent place. He received approval to work and continued working until 19:00. For working around eight hours, he received 270 *birr*. As he aimed to earn more money, he asked *Wanna*-A for permission and worked in the night shift in other days; thus, he was able to work on two days (the 22nd and the 25th). YB-L's case of searching for part-time work opportunities showed that there was a possibility of YBs being instantly employed by visiting the terminal.

Table 15. Working schedule of Group Z and YB-L's earnings (November 18 to 25, 2019)

Schedule	Time	Date			
		Nov 18	Nov 20	Nov 22	Nov 25
Shift-1	6:00 - 12:00	YB-E YB-M	YB-E YB-M	YB-E YB-M	YB-E YB-M
Shift-2	12:00 - 15:00	YB-F YB-G	YB-F **YB-L** **(140 *birr*)**	YB-F YB-G	YB-F YB-G
Shift-3	15:00 - 20:00	*n.d.*	YB-F **YB-L** **(130 *birr*)**	YB-*n.d.* **YB-L** **(130 *birr*)**	YB-*n.d.* **YB-L** **(100 *birr*, 15:00-17:00)**

Source: Author's fieldwork.

Instability of tera askebari labor market: Weekly schedule of Platform X

How successfully can YBs obtain part-time opportunities? Table 16 shows the schedule of Groups Y and Z, from October 14 to 18, 2019. The letters in black ink indicate the YBs who were working regularly. Although nine YBs were designated for the regular position, the unemployed YBs still had a chance to obtain part-time opportunities. That is, during the absence of regular workers and during the workers' mealtimes, YBs who visited the terminal could obtain work opportunities.

First, in the case of Group Z, the regular workers were YB-A and YB-E (shift-1 [6:00 to 12:00]), YB-F and YB-G (shift-2 [12:00 to 15:00]), and YB-F and YB-L (shift-3 [15:00 to 20:00]). On October 14, six unemployed YBs visited the terminal. Among them, two YBs, YB-N and YB-K, were able to obtain work opportunities because of the absence of regular workers. On October 16th, five YBs visited the terminal, but none of them was able to get employed, while YB-H got work opportunities on 18th.

In the case of Group Y, the forms of employment were different from Group Z which was hiring regular workers from morning to 18:30. YB-A, B, C, and D were hired in the regular position and all of them attended to work. While there were no seats for unemployed YBs to work for the regular worker's vacancy, there was a chance for them to get part-time opportunities. On October 15th and 17th, YB-U and YB-V worked on the regular worker's breakfast time. On their lunchtime, YB-R worked on 15th and YB-P worked on 17th. The night-time shift of Group Y was operating on an ad-hoc hiring basis. YB-M and YB-Q could work on the 15th and 17th respectively.

In five days, the number of unemployed YBs visiting Platform X ranged from five to nine people per day. However, the success rate of their search for work ranged from 0% to 62.5%. This value shows that the chances of unemployed YBs obtaining work opportunities were erratic. It means that the *tera askebari* labor market had a high degree of variability and uncertainty in terms of work opportunities. What then is the reason for YBs' continuous visits to Platform X?

Table 16. Weekly schedule of Platform X (October 14 to 18, 2019)

Time \ Date	Mon 14	Tue 15	Wed 16	Thurs 17	Fri 18
6~9	A, E	A, B, C, D	A, E	A, B, C, D	A, E
9~12	A, E	10:15 U, V	A, E	11:03 U, V	A, E
12~15	F, N	15:24	F, G	14:40 P	F, G
15~18	L, K	R	F, L	Q	F, H
18~21	L, K	M	F, L	Q	F, H
Visited	6	6	5	9	5
Selected	2	4	0	4	1
Success Rate	33.3%	66.6%	0%	44.4%	20%

Note: Alphabet with the black letter are YBs in regular position and the red letters are YBs who worked part-time.

Diversifying work opportunities to other transport work

The *tera askebari* work at Platform X was somewhat unstable. The YBs' employment contract is made verbally and this condition sometimes makes it challenging for YBs to earn their livelihoods. Although some of the YBs enter into regular contracts with managers or *wanna*, this does not mean that their seats are permanent. Their contracts are verbal and informal, and they can be easily dismissed from service. To cope with the uncertain and unstable working environment of Platform X, YBs diversify their working choices instead of solely depending on the *tera askebari* work.

Terminal as a social place

Platform X was not only a place for managing the minibuses but also a social meeting point where YBs could interact and form a personal network with other minibus-related workers. By visiting the terminal, YBs increased their chances of communicating with minibus workers (drivers minibus attendants). The YBs had high chances of interacting with minibus workers during the *medebegna gize* (period before the rush hour could start. See Chapter 7 for details.) Most vehicles were waiting for approximately 20 to 30 minutes to fill the passengers and depart. This long time-interval enabled the YBs and minibus workers to communicate and construct personal relationships with each other.

When YBs had some spare time, they entered the empty minibuses and chatted with the drivers. For some time, they often talked with drivers while sitting near the driver's seat. The drivers would often exit their vehicles to do some stretching, smoke tobacco, and chat with the YBs. They shared some information about incidents that had occurred in the terminal, information about the traffic and the existence of the traffic police, and so on. This personal network between the YBs and the minibus workers formed an important knowledge source for the YBs to expand their work opportunities.

Working as minibus attendant

First, it provided them with a chance to work as attendants. When there was a vacancy, drivers would often ask YBs to work with them or ask them to introduce them to a trustworthy worker. For example, YB-C had been working under Mgr-B in a regular position. He was working in the terminal for about one year. One day, he quarreled with Mgr-B (January 16, 2020). Being infuriated, Mgr-B asked him not to come to the terminal on the next day. Mgr-B hired a substitute, YB-M, to work in YB-C's position. Despite YB-C losing his job in a second, he was able to find other work the next day. He called some drivers in his contacts and found one vacancy to work as an attendant and he was able to start the work on the next day (January 17, 2020).

Working as lamera

Characteristics of lamera

The other work position available to YBs was that of *lamera*. *Lamera* are minibus touts who help minibus drivers and attendant by touting the passengers at the terminal. They are not always present in every terminal, but they are often found working at places where collecting passengers is difficult. They assist drivers in touting to passengers faster, both in the presence and in the absence of attendant. Their name is derived from a supplement that supports the cement of the building in construction, as they support the drivers. The major difference between assistant and *lamera* is that, while assistants work with the driver as a team, the *lamera* works individually and makes contracts based on the demands of the driver. If the drivers do not want the *lamera* to work for them, they do not hire them.

According to the *tera askebari* in Platform X, the work of *lamera* started around eight years ago to support minibuses working on the Bole Arabsa route. Since 2016, condominiums have been built in the Bole Arabsa area, and only midi-sized *higher* buses and *k'etk'et* buses have been allowed to operate in this area. However, due to growing demand, minibuses have also begun to operate here. It was illegal to take a minibus, but people started to use minibus services, as they were providing faster services. Accordingly, Platform X started the service of the Bole Arabsa route, as well as the work of *lamera*. The work position of *lamera* began naturally in order to support drivers who were picking up passengers with the suggestions of the YBs who often visited the terminal and spent time there. While it is the driver's choice to collect the passengers, most of the drivers hired YBs as *lamera* because touting a destination was not an easy job. *Lamera* received 10 *birr* when they filled one vehicle to capacity. Due to easy access, these activities have become one of the major choices for YBs and helped them to survive in times of unemployment.

Table 17. Working shift of *lamera* (October 10, 2019)

Worker	Start time	End time	Time interval
YB-N	11:03	11:15	12'
YB-O	11:15	11:35	20'
YB-P	11:35	11:55	20'
YB-N	11:55	12:20	25'
YB-O	12:20	12:30	10'
YB-O	12:30	12:40	10'
YB-P	12:40	13:05	25'
YB-N	13:05	13:15	10'
YB-O	13:15	13:50	35'
YB-P	13:50	14:05	15'

Source: Author's own observation.

Table 17 shows the timetable of the *lamera* on October 10, 2019. The time interval is ranges from 10 to 35 minutes. The sequence of the worker is N-O-P, but O has worked two times from 12:20 to 12:40. There may be some reason that the O has not gain enough working opportunities last night or he needs little more money. This shows that YBs who works for the *lamera* are arranging their working sequence by their own rules.

They were able to work for shorter periods and quit whenever they wanted. As an example, YB-N came to the terminal at approximately 10:30 a.m. He worked three times for approximately 2 hours and 12 minutes. The frequency of the vehicles at Bole Arabsa was as follows: around four vehicles passed by in an hour. Under these conditions, YBs—always three or four of them—came to the terminal and were able to receive work opportunities. In the case of YB-N, he would typically start working at 11:03 and finish his work at 13:15. The net-working time was 47 minutes, and the total working time including waiting time was 2 hour 12 minutes. As *lamera* work's earnings for one vehicle was 10 *birr*, and totally he earned 30 *birr*. After working for a short time, he returned home.

YB-D and YB-N's case

YB-D was working as a *tera askebari* for about one and a half years. One day, he quarreled with Mgr-B over some issues and stopped working (November 19, 2019). However, the dismissal from the *tera askebari* work did not mean that YB-D remained unemployed. He was able to find work as a *lamera* after the day he was dismissed. He started to work as a *lamera* from November 20 onward for three days and worked as an attendant after that. He could easily alternate between *lamera* and attendant work because of the experiences and networks he had formed in this community. He knew most of the YBs and drivers who were working in the Bole Arabsa route, and this enabled him to transfer to *lamera* work. YB-D's case shows that their long-term experience in the transport sector enabled YBs to receive less shocks when they faced a crisis; that is, they were simply able to transfer their position to other types of work within allied professions.

Many unemployed YBs visited the terminal and were able to obtain work opportunities, working as *tera askebari*, attendant, or *lamera*, depending on the situation. Despite the precarious situation of such occupations, the experiences and networks that YBs accumulated in this community helped them to easily shift to similar occupations when they faced employment problems. Thus, under the uncertain conditions of informal transport work, YBs were able to diversify their work choices, and these activities enabled them to increase their earning opportunities and survivability.

Advancing to the next life stage

The Terminal Community was often a steppingstone toward a higher level of living. For example, YB-A (in his mid-20s) aimed to become a minibus driver to obtain better economic opportunities. YB-A started working as a *tera askebari* in Group Z in 2017. He was first introduced to this line of work by a former YB. At first, he worked only during the morning shift (6:00 to 12:00) in this group and received 100 *birr* as a wage. YB-A initially had no strong willingness to expand his working time. He said he used his earnings for spending time at the *ch'at* house,[5] chewing *ch'at*, and smoking cigarettes and shisha—in short, spending time meaninglessly. One day, he realized that he had not gained anything but a tired body after a year of such activities. His family was highly dependent on his earnings. Except for YB-A, no other family members were engaged in economic activities. YB-A aimed to become a minibus driver so as to earn a better income and obtain stable work. Usually, minibus drivers' daily earning ranged from 400 to 600 *birr*, which is higher than the job of *tera askebari*. As he wanted to work more, he requested Mgr-A to let him work under him as well. In August 2018, Mgr-A accepted YB-A, so he was able to work in both Groups Y and Z. By doing two types of regular work, YB-A's salary increased dramatically. While his weekly salary in 2017 was 300 *birr*, he earned 960 *birr* a week in 2019. By working almost every day, YB-A was able to finance his driving school fees of 12,000 *birr* for three months of training. During my fieldwork, he took a driving class three times a week from 14:00 to 15:00 after finishing the Group Z's morning shift. In other words, he used his spare time in self-development to become a driver. Thus, for YB-A, the *tera askebari* work was not only a means of earning money but also a platform that allowed him to move closer to fulfilling the dream of his future and move on to a better stage of life.

In another case study as well, the work of *tera askebari* was found to be a steppingstone for the YBs to move to another stage of life. YB-K had been working as a part-time worker for many years. YB-K came to the terminal casually and negotiated work opportunities with managers or *wanna*. He would occasionally come to the terminal and seek work. For example, in September, he worked three times irregularly (Sep, 13: 8:00-12:00, Sep, 14: 13:00-15:00, Sep, 16: 12:00-15:00). It was found that YB-K was preparing to start a new business for used-phone brokerage and *bajaji* (ባጃጅ, tricycle) retail. For him, the *tera askebari* work did not just provide a place to stay but also a steppingstone toward starting his own business.

If the YBs were lucky, they could receive a chance of becoming a manager in the *tera askebari* business. For example, Mgr-B started working as part-time worker 13 years ago. By working honestly, he won the recognition of the *wanna* and was able to step up to a manager-level position. While his was a rare case, Mgr-B's case showed that there is a possibility to occupy the higher *tera askebari* position. In summary, the *tera askebari* work was not only a means of survival but also a platform for some YBs, which helped them move to the next stage of their lives.

Summary

Chapter 5 provided observations regarding the livelihoods and coping strategies of YBs who are working and finding job opportunities at Platform X. The *tera askebari* work at Platform X was in a weak labor environment. Their employment contract is made verbally, and this condition sometimes challenged the YBs. Although some of the YBs enter into regular contracts with managers or *wanna*, this does not mean that their seats are permanent. Their contracts are made verbal and informal, and they can be easily dismissed from service. Under this high employment instability, YBs expanded their viability by diversifying the work opportunities. By interacting vigorously with the minibus workers, they broaden the opportunities from the work of *tera askebari* to attendant and *lamera*. Meanwhile, their strategies were not confined to this terminal. The Terminal Community was an option for them, and they tried to find other kinds of job vigorously, which helps them to increase their survivability to live in this city. In other words, YB's strategies to keep connected with Terminal Community and their attitudes and activities to acquire and transfer to different kinds of opportunities clearly indicate that they are neither precarious nor vulnerable, but has a potential to develop their own career. They were subjective entities who have power to lead their own lives and who can layout suitable strategies to cope with the rapidly changing African urban labor market.

Notes

[1] A word which combines "precarious" and "proletariat."

[2] Shola (ሾላ) refers to a Sycamore fig tree (*Ficus sycomorus*) that is grown in the Southern part of Africa. The place name of Gurd Shola (ጉርድ ሾላ) refers to a Shola tree that was cut off; the name origin story refers to a big Shola tree that was cut off a long time ago.

[3] Interview of officer at *woreda* 7 (September 25, 2019).

[4] A holiday which commemorates the discovery of True Cross in Ethiopian Orthodox.

[5] *Ch'at bet* (ጫት ቤት) is a place where people gather and chew *ch'at* (khat). Ch'at is a green plant containing stimulant drugs which speed up the mind and body.

Chapter 6. *Tera Askebari*'s Management Activities and Their Social Roles

Introduction

It is unquestionable on the role played by informal transport in Africa. Despite this fact, transport workers in Africa have been portrayed negatively for a long time, academically as well as socially. There have been prevailing negative views on the characteristics of the informal transport workers. First, they have often been stereotyped as "aggressive" and "violent," bothered only with maximizing their profits rather than the passengers' demands (Mobereola 2009: 3; Davison 2019: 70). Second, transport workers were relegated as socially marginalized, as their origins, such as lack of education and migrant background, have contributed on created negative perceptions towards them (Fekadu 2014: 124-125; Tilahun 2014: 124). Furthermore, they were portrayed as incompetent in various aspects, such as having difficulties to get a job or precarious to be easily impacted by state forces and the exploitative system (Rizzo 2011: 1200; Doherty 2017). They have been defined in negative ways, such as "young men in impossible positions" (Mbugua 2013: 212), "precariats" (Siyabulela 2021: 145), or "disposable people" (Doherty 2017), who are unable to solve their own problems. However, this pervasive negative portrayal of transport workers impeded our understanding of their abilities and the crucial roles they played in the public services sector, making it difficult for us to understand their full potential.

Tera askebari in Addis Ababa have been providing transport management services since 1980s. Notwithstanding *tera askebari*'s significant role in the urban transport system, there have been pervasive negative views about *tera askebari*, both socially and academically. *Tera askebari* has been portrayed as a vagabond and misbehaved person (Fekadu 2013: 69), those who use street violence (Di Nunzio 2012: 440), and who utilize money for personal purposes (AACCSA 2009: 177-178). This pervasive negative image of *tera askebari* hindered the proper assessment of their activities. Their management methods were simply treated as unmethodical and have not received proper attention (AACCSA 2009: 178). In general, there has been a lack of academic interest in understanding the roles of *tera askebari* in society.

As further research is required on the above subject, I examine the *tera askebari*'s roles and contributions in society based on their practices and processes in managing the vehicles and passengers at minibus terminals in Addis Ababa. I also observe the passengers' perceptions of *tera askebari* in order to analyze the research question in a balanced manner. This chapter examines three research questions. First, what are the two sessions in *tera askebari*'s activities and how do they vary? Second, what is the quality of words and phrases they use in their activities? Third, what are the passengers' perceptions of *tera askebari*?

This study mainly focuses on *tera askebari*'s activities in the western section of Platform X. Nonetheless, the part examining their language use considers their activities in the eastern section as well. Although most *tera askebari* in this field are from the Hadiya and Wolaytta ethnic groups (for details see Chapter 6), the common language they use is Amharic, a lingua franca in Addis Ababa. Thus, I conducted interviews in Amharic and translated their utterances into English.

Characteristics of *tera askebari* business in Platform X

Tera askebari basically earn their income from minibuses. They guide the minibuses in queuing up and direct them to move when the vehicles in front depart. For providing these services, they receive *sadi* (a *tera askebari* service charge) from the minibus operators who utilize the terminal. The *sadi* amount varies by minibus destination and is calculated according to the amount of money a minibus driver earns for each trip (as it is explained in Table 12). For example, the shortest route at this terminal is the Gurd Shola route. The passenger fare for this route is 1.5 *birr*, and *tera askebari* collect 5 *birr* as *sadi* per vehicle in this route. The *sadi* for most routes (Semit, Semit Condominium, Ayat, Ayat Ch'afe, and T'afo) is 7 *birr*, with the passenger fares ranging from 4.5 to 7.5 *birr*. Although the distance of the Bole Arabsa route does not differ significantly from that of T'afo, the *sadi* for this route is 20 *birr*. This is because the *sadi* that *tera askebari* collect for each route is based on the revenue the minibuses earn at the terminal, rather than the distance of the route. The AARTB does not permit minibuses to operate on the Bole Arabsa route even though there is always a high demand for transportation due to a large condominium complex at its final destination. Therefore, despite being illegal, many minibuses operate on this route, with the drivers not hesitating to take in even twenty passengers per vehicle, that is, five to eight more than the regulated number. As minibuses on the Bole Arabsa route collected comparatively higher revenue than those playing on other routes, *tera askebari* collected higher *sadi* in this route.

Tera askebari's activities in handling the minibuses

Tera askebari's activities at medebegna gize

In this terminal, the *tera askebari*'s activities are largely classified into two categories based on the number of passengers. The first is the regular hour activities, in which the passengers do not line up in a queue, and the other is rush hour activities, in which the passengers usually line up at the terminal. Depending on this classification, the *tera askebari*'s major roles and activities show variances.

The first classification is called *medebegna gize* (መደበኛ ጊዜ, normal time), and the second one is called *ayer saat* (አየር ሰዓት, rush hour). The term *medebegna* (መደበኛ) means basic, regular, or ordinary, while *gize* (ጊዜ) refers to the time (Kane 1990 Vol. 1: 328). In this terminal, tera askebari refer to the "ordinary time that is not busy or not having special tasks" as *medebegna gize*.[1] This time ranges from the start of business hours (5:30 or 6:00) to the start of passengers lining up (between 15:40 to 17:00).

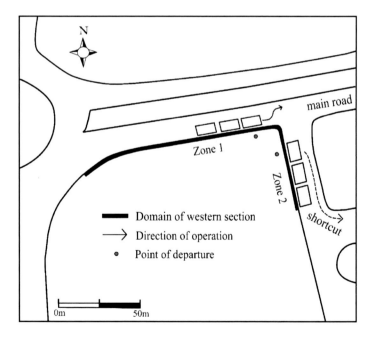

Figure 32. Aerial view of the Western section, Platform X

At *medebegna gize*, the number of minibuses was more than the number of passengers. Also, there were many minibuses waiting to depart, so the minibus operation functioned under two zones. In Figure 32, the black line drawn along the road indicates the domain controlled by *tera askebari*. Here, minibuses operate to two destinations, Semit and Semit Condominium. Minibuses operating to these destinations work jointly in zones 1 and 2, without strict separation, because these lines share common operating routes. The only difference between zones 1 and 2 lies in the roads that the vehicles use. Vehicles operating in zone 1 use the main road, as allowed by the AARTB, passing by the Yetebaberut roundabout.[2] Those operating in zone 2 share the same destinations with the vehicles operating in zone 1, but take shortcuts through the Figa roundabout.[3] Minibuses taking shortcuts travel relatively faster as there are not many signals and traffic jams, but have fewer opportunities to collect passengers while using shortcut roads. From the study so far, minibus drivers choose their zone to work depending on the traffic condition at that time.

In this time zone, minibuses have a long waiting time, which impacts the *tera askebari*'s activities (see Figures 33). The average dispatch interval in the western section was around 2 minutes 20 seconds, based on the interview conducted with YB-A on September 18, 2019. The total earnings from 7 a.m. to 12 p.m. on that day was 930 *birr*, with average hourly earnings of 186 *birr* (930/5h = 186 *birr*). Assuming the normal *sadi* as 7 *birr* per vehicle, we find that 26.6 fleets depart from this terminal in an hour (186 *birr*/7 *birr* = 26.6 fleets), with minibuses showing a waiting time of 2 minutes 20 seconds. Normally, 8 to 10 vehicles are found waiting at each zone at a time, indicating that a vehicle's waiting time ranged from approximately 15 to 30 minutes. Due to the number of vehicles, some minibus operators try to collect passengers without queuing up, so the *tera askebari*'s main job is to maintain the order of minibuses.

There were two terminologies which refer to minibus workers who queue up and those who try to break the order. The former operators are called *teregna* (ተረኛ, queuer),[4] meaning a person in a row and in order. In contrast, several minibus operators disregard the order and barge into or cut the line. These are minibus operators who want to compete in collecting passengers faster. These operators are called *tebareri* (ተባሪሪ, one who flee),[5] and their breach activities are called *efem* (አፈም, foul) or foul (ፋውል) among themselves. Based on the consensus between *tera askebari* and minibus operators with regard to queuing up, *tera askebari* are required to take measures against *tebareri*'s breach. In this terminal, *tera askebari* respond differently and take different measures on the *tebareri*'s action.

Figure 33. Platform X at *medebegna gize* (October 5, 2019, 2:55 p.m.)

Expel the tebareri

The major activity of *tera askebari* in the *medebegna gize* is to maintain the order of minibuses in the queue. This gives them the responsibility of not only securing the order of minibuses, but also prohibiting and preventing minibus workers from trying to break the rules. The first measure they take is to expel the offending *tebareri*. For instance, consider this case. One day, minibus no. 133 barges in at the back of zone 1 and starts to tout passengers (see Figure 34). Minibus no. 133 did not queue up before touting passengers, nor did the operator get any consent from the *tera askebari*. The operator could obtain five passengers before this was discovered by one *tera askebari*, YB-A.[6] YB-A went directly to the vehicle and questioned the attendant. YB-A then opened the door and asked the passengers to cooperate, by saying "Sorry, please move to the front vehicle." After that, all the passengers alighted from the vehicle and moved to the vehicle which was in front of the queue. YB-A slammed the door of no. 133 and did not allow it to operate (August 30, 2019). This case shows *tera askebari* were prohibiting *tebareri* to collect passengers. Minibus no. 133 tried to collect passengers without the *tera askebari* noticing. Since they directly confronted the *tera askebari*'s power, the latter responded by not allowing them to operate the business.

Charging derebo

On the other case, *tera askebari* charge higher *sadi* rather than chase the offending minibuses. Imposing a higher *sadi* was another measure to protect *teregna*; this is referred to as *derebo*. One day, YB-B sat at the handrails of a pedestrian road to monitor the minibuses. While observing the minibuses in his territory, he also monitored the vehicles on the western side. When he observed several *tebareri* committing *efem*, he ran to the spot and confronted the minibus workers directly, saying "whoa, whoa, whoa...... *aba*,[7] you know it is forbidden to stop here," and "You, do not park your car here twice." He warned them that he would not allow them to operate in this terminal if they commit *efem* again. He charged 10 *birr* of *derebo* to seven vehicles who operate in this area (October 15, 2019).

The minibuses operating in this spot were taking a risk because the *tera askebari*'s power were scarcely reaching this point. The *tera askebari*'s sphere of action is mostly near the minibuses in queue (Figure 34). Therefore, many minibuses commit *efem* outside this point in order to obtain passengers faster, without queuing up or paying *sadi* to the *tera askebari*. At this time, imposing a higher *sadi* was a measure to penalize the *tebareri* and business rights of the teregna in their operating zone.

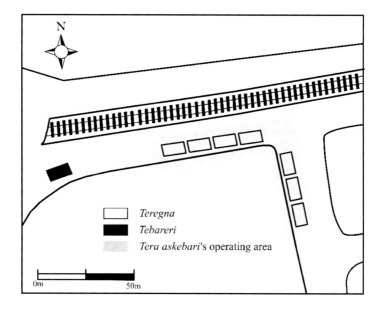

Figure 34. *Tera askebari*'s main operating area and the place where YB-B caught the seven *tebareri*

Permit the tebareri to operate secretly

One day, YB-T was working as minibus attendant in a part-time job. While heading to Semit, he collected 10 passengers from other terminals, and few seats were left. Meanwhile, YB-A was sitting on a chair near street vendors, monitoring vehicles in the western section. Approaching the end of the queue in zone 1, YB-T sent a signal to YB-A to allow him a few passengers. YB-A then returned the signal, first pointing 1 and then 2 fingers, asking YB-T whether he could collect a few passengers. YB-T answered by showing a V-shape, implying that two seats were left. YB-A then checked the situation in the terminal and granted permission by nodding his head. While approaching, YB-T touts with a low voice, asking people whether they were going to the destination. Two passengers nodded and got into the vehicle. In this case, YB-A permitted YB-T to operate secretly by prioritizing his personal relations over duty. Meanwhile, he did not want to be recognized by other operators in the queue. Although he failed in his duty to protect the *teregna*, his discreet attitude indicated that he was trying to protect the order of minibuses in the terminal.

Permit the tebareri regardless of opposition

In certain cases, *tera askebari* permit the *teregna* to operate regardless of opposition from other workers. Consider this case as an example. Minibus no. 237 barged into the front of the queue in the middle of zones 1 and 2, trying to operate in the western section (Figure 35). Many *teregna* complained and asked the *tera askebari* to intervene in the situation. However, the *tera askebari* disregarded the complaints of the operators and condoned the *efem* of no. 237. Rolling his eyes, the *tera askebari* mumbled, "It's okay, just once." Furthermore, he did not collect any *sadi* or *derebo* (September 6, 2019). Similar cases in which *tera askebari* secretly approve specific minibus operators committing *efem* occur occasionally. This happened when *tera askebari* prioritize their personal relations with acquaintances rather than their duties. Meanwhile, such activities cause opposition or resistance from *teregna* as the *tera askebari* directly breaches the mutual agreements between *teregna*. Moreover, if they continue to permit their acquaintances to commit *efem*, there was possibility that minibus operators might look down upon the *tera askebari*'s ability, which would make their terminal's reputation as an "easy working place." Thus, granting permission despite the other operators' opposition was highly risky with respect to their authority, which was not frequently happened.

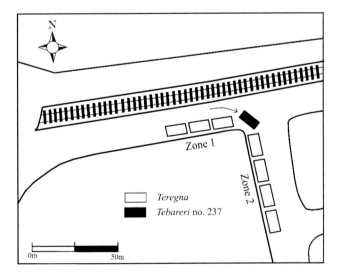

Figure 35. Place where minibus no. 237 barged in

Tera askebari's activities at ayer saat

The other category was rush hour, which was called *ayer saat* (አየር ሰዓት).[8] The term *ayer* (አየር) means atmosphere or weather, and *saat* (ሰዓት) means time. Minibus workers use the term *ayer* to refer to "a flux of passengers." Thus, *ayer saat* refers to the time when a large number of passengers gather at the terminal.

In this terminal, a queue was usually formed between 16:00 and 17:00. Usually, the government office hour is 8:30 to 17:30 in Ethiopia. Meanwhile, the cause of passenger jam in *ayer saat* seems to be caused by the demand of passengers who leave their work earlier and also the passengers going back to home. Two destinations in the western section, Semit and Semit Condominium, have large residential complexes. Many commuters working in the central part of the city use this terminal to return to their homes. Thus, a long queue forms in the late afternoon as many passengers returning to their homes gather at the terminals (Figures 36). Here, unlike in *medebegna gize*, which is divided into two zones, all the vehicles form a single queue in zone 2. This is because all minibuses usually take shortcuts to their destinations to avoid heavy traffic on the main road and most passengers utilize this service to go directly to their destinations.

Figure 36. Passengers lining up at *ayer saat* (October 25, 2019, 5:02 p.m.)

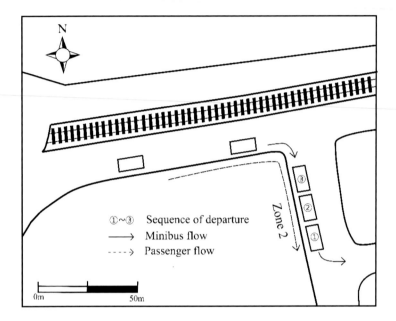

Figure 37. Flow of minibuses and passenger queue at *ayer saat*

In the *ayer saat*, as the passenger's demand was higher than the number of minibuses, the minibuses waiting time was shorter than the *medebegna gize*. The flow of departure is fast as the average dispatch interval of a fleet is only about 1 minute and 5.4 seconds. On September 3, passengers started to line up from 15:50, and this continued until the *tera askebari* finished their work at 18:30. Within 2 hours and 39 minutes, 145 vehicles departed from the terminal. In one hour, 54.7 vehicles on average departed from the terminal, meaning that one vehicle's dispatch interval was about 1 minute and 5.4 seconds. Similarly, the average waiting time of a vehicle in the eastern section was 45.86 seconds (Table 18). Compared with *medebegna gize*, where the waiting time is approximately 2 minutes and 20 seconds, the waiting time in *ayer saat* is shorter, indicating a faster flow of minibus departure.

The role of *tera askebari* at this time was to manage minibuses and passengers and provide them with quick service. First, their role was to assist passengers rapidly by counting the number of passengers. For example, on September 3, 2019 at 17:03, Mgr-A commanded YB-A to count the number of passengers with the words, "*K'ut'aru, k'ut'aru* (ቁጥሩ, ቁጥሩ, count, count)," an order to count the number of passengers. YB-A counted 16 passengers and then told the passengers which vehicle they should board. This method helps to prioritize passengers in the queue.

Meanwhile, there were some passengers who cut in line and try to enter the vehicle without queueing. This created a jam at the minibus entrance. In this situation, *tera askebari* filled the regular seats to the passengers who were in the queue and allotted the spare seats to those who jumped the line. Spare seats refer to informal seats that are usually made with wood board or automobile parts, so it was not preferred by most of the passengers. Thus, *tera askebari* first filled the queuers and then allotted the spare seats to queue jumper, and it was a method to board passengers faster and assist those in the queue to gain priority.

In *ayer saat*, one of the major factors influencing *tera askebari*'s activities is the existence of transport workers called *tek'ot'at'eri*. They are public servants sent by AARTB to check whether minibuses are operating on the allotted route. Two workers are sent to the terminal in two shifts in a day, one in the morning (6:00 to 12:00) and the other in the afternoon (12:00 to 18:00). Minibus drivers are required to obtain a stamp from the *tek'ot'at'eri* when they complete three round-trips in one shift (Figure 38). Whereas *tek'ot'at'eri* normally visit the terminal late in the afternoon (around 16:00 to 18:00) and affix a seal even if the drivers operated only one trip from the terminal. In this manner, *tek'ot'at'eri* shorten their work hours. While *tek'ot'at'eri* visit a terminal in both *medebegna gize* and the *ayer saat*, they have a larger impact on *ayer saat* as there would be a large number of passengers and minibuses trying to depart rapidly.

Tek'ot'at'eri usually stand in the middle of the western and eastern sections and sign the attendance sheet when the driver brings it to them, as shown in Figure 39. However, if a driver has not worked in the assigned route, he will have to pay a fine of 200 *birr*, which often leads to some altercation between *tek'ot'at'eri* and the drivers. Even if they are keeping the passengers waiting, the drivers are required to get the *tek'ot'at'eri*'s signatures; meanwhile *tera askebari* have to manage the minibuses and maintain order in such situations. *Tera askebari*'s major role in this time were thus, not only to support passengers and drivers to depart rapidly but also judge what is best based on the circumstances.

Table 18. Number of operating vehicles in Eastern section at *ayer saat*

Number of vehicles	Time-lapse	Time span	Number of vehicles	Time-lapse	Time span
1	0'00"	1:08	37	0'35"	34:37
2	0'32"	1:40	38	0'30"	35:07
3	1'38"	3:18	39	0'01"	35:08
4	0'11"	3:29	40	0'11"	35:19
5	0'23"	3:52	41	0'03"	35:22
6	0'56"	4:48	42	0'37"	35:59
7	1'03"	5:51	43	0'13"	36:12
8	0'35"	6:26	44	0'00"	36:12
9	0'39"	7:05	45	0'03"	36:15
10	2'32"	9:37	46	0'32"	36:47
11	0'53"	10:30	47	0'17"	37:04
12	0'41"	11:11	48	1'19"	38:23
13	0'32"	11:43	49	0'11"	38:34
14	1'02"	12:45	50	0'30"	39:04
15	2'20"	15:05	51	1'09"	40:13
16	0'35"	15:40	52	0'59"	41:12
17	0'28"	16:08	53	0'01"	41:13
18	0'52"	17:00	54	0'50"	42:03
19	0'14"	17:14	55	0'00"	42:03
20	0'57"	18:11	56	0'01"	42:04
21	2'37"	20:48	57	0'08"	42:12
22	0'15"	21:03	58	0'04"	42:16
23	0'20"	21:23	59	1'04"	43:20
24	1'27"	22:50	60	1'47"	45:07
25	1'34"	24:24	61	0'02"	45:09
26	0'33"	24:57	62	0'55"	46:04
27	3'22"	28:19	63	0'11"	46:15
28	0'02"	28:21	64	0'58"	47:13
29	2'32"	30:53	65	1'47"	49:00
30	0'37"	31:30	66	0'05"	49:05
31	0'17"	31:47	67	0'45"	49:50
32	0'15"	32:02	68	0'45"	50:35
33	0'04"	32:06	69	1'23"	51:58
34	0'29"	32:35	70	1'04"	53:02
35	0'12"	32:47	71	1'56"	54:58
36	1'14"	34:02	72	0'04"	55:02

Source: Author's observation in the 2019 fieldwork.

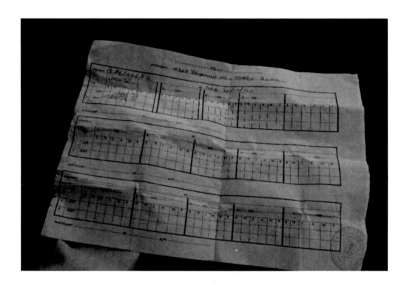

Figure 38. Attendance sheet of minibus driver (September 2, 2019, 6:32 a.m.)

Two types of scenes showed the flexible management of *tera askebari* in *ayer saat*. The first is *tera askebari*'s attempts to maintain the order of minibuses. On September 10, 2019, at 16:32 a minibus driver in the first row was talking with a public servant from the transport authority. As their conversation extended for about two minutes, Mgr-A approached them to find out the reason. The problem was that the driver did not get the required signature a few days earlier. Mgr-A supported the driver, saying that he must have forgotten and thus tried to appease the transport worker. Meanwhile, three minibuses and approximately one hundred passengers were waiting for Mgr-A's permission. Once the problem was solved, Mgr-A told to workers, "*mejemmeriya ch'an, ch'an* (መጀመሪያ ጫን ጫን, load first)," giving them permission to let the passengers enter the vehicles at the front of the queue. On the other case, one minibus operator's conversation with the transport worker was prolonged more than 5 minutes, and in the middle, *tera askebari* did not wait for him but embarked passengers to other minibuses who were at the back of the queue (September 10, 2019, 17:56). As more time had elapsed than expected, the *tera askebari* judged that allowing passengers to enter vehicles faster was more important than maintaining the queue.

Figure 39. Two *tek'ot'et'ari* and the drivers trying to get the signature in the middle of the Western and the Eastern sections (August 29, 2019, 6:47 a.m.)

Words and phrases in tera askebari's activities

Imperative form

Observation 1: October 12, 2019, 13:36. Eastern section

Unlike the western section, which operated in only two destinations, the eastern section had five destinations, and so this section was often crowded with minibuses. On October 12, 2019, at the observation time, many minibuses that had to go to different destinations gathered at the terminal and caused a heavy traffic jam. When Mgr-B noticed this situation, he ordered the minibuses to move, saying "*Eza, t'ega belu* (እዛ, ጥጋ በሉ)."[9] This means, "There, narrow down the gap between each other" (Table 19).

Table 19. Expression which *tera askebari* uses when controlling the minibuses

Phrase	Amharic	Meaning
Asgeba	አስገባ	Let the minibuses / passengers in
Aswut'awu	አስወጣው	Take it (your vehicles) out
Asmola	አስሞላ	Let it (the vehicles) be filled with the passengers
T'aga bel	ጥጋ በል	Narrow the gap between the minibuses
K'es belo	ቀስ ብሎ	Take it slowly or act slowly
Hid	ሂድ	Go, depart
Lash bel	ላሽ በል	Go away
Zor bel	ዞር በል	Go away
Sebiyo	ሰቢዮ	Go away
Ch'an	ጫን	Load
Elef	እለፍ	Pass
Sab	ሳብ	Depart
Enka	እንካ	Take it
Atchan	አትጫን	Do not fill the passengers
Atk'om	አትቆም	Do not park here

Source: Author's observation in the 2019 fieldwork.

Observation 2: October 10, 2019, 14:20. Eastern section

One minibus was trying to collect passengers to Gurd Shola without obtaining permission from the *tera askebari*.[10] YB-C and YB-D told him not to conduct the trip, but the attendant continued to call out to passengers for the destination. One senior *tera askebari* who noticed the incident told the attendant, "*Ante, k'es belo* (አንተ, ቀስ ብለው)," which meant "You, take it slowly."

Observation 3: October 15, 2019. Western section

YB-B seated at the handrail of the pedestrian road was monitoring vehicles on the western side. When he found a *tebareri* collecting passengers without permission, he rushed to the spot directly and told the *tebareri*, "*Ezih gar atk'om* (እዚህ ጋር አትቆም)," which means "Do not stop (your vehicle) here."

The *tera askebari*'s utterances in Observations 1 and 2 consisted with address form and the imperative verb form. Mgr-B called the minibus workers "there." Thereafter, he ordered them to narrow the gap between each other. In the next observation, the senior *tera askebari* called the opponent "*ante*," which is a direct address, meaning "you," and then ordered the attendant to act slowly. The *tera askebari*'s utterance in Observation 3 was a negative imperative, which was a command not to carry out a certain activity.

The *tera askebari*'s way of ordering was often observed at other times as well. Once in *ayer saat* (September 24, 2019, at 16:59), an attendant who had collected 17 passengers was trying to collect one more saying, "Is there one person?" The *tera askebari* told him, "*Bek'a, hid bek'a* (በቃ, ሂድ በቃ)," which means "Enough, go enough," and slammed the door. In other cases, they say *elef,* to drive away minibuses; "*sab*" to order minibuses to depart; or "*chan*" to embark passengers.

These utterances indicate two social aspects. First, the addressee form is short (*eza, ante*) and clearly mention the specific addressees. Second, the communication is a directive. They do not consist of interrogatives or declaratives, such as "could you narrow the gap?" or "I request you not to park here," but rather imperative commands delivered straight to the minibus workers. These characteristics arise from the social environment of the urban transport sectors in which *tera askebari* are required to manage hundreds of vehicles daily along crowded roads. By using short and direct utterances, *tera askebari* can convey their power and authority to minibus workers more rapidly and efficiently. However, their imperative way of talking does not always demonstrate a higher status compared to minibus workers. This is because the imperative tone is often used by other minibus workers as well.

Observation 6: September 13, 2019, 15:37. Ayat terminal

On September 13, 2019, I observed the behavior of a minibus attendant. As soon as he arrived at the Ayat terminal, he greeted the *tera askebari* saying, "*Selam* (ሰላም)." After collecting enough passengers, he give 5 *birr* to the *tera askebari* saying, "*Enka* (እንካ)," which means "Take it."

The phrase "*enka*" is an imperative verb used when speaking to people of a lower status. This phrase is used not only when minibus attendants speak to *tera askebari,* but also when attendants speak to passengers, passengers speak to attendants, and *tera askebari* speak to attendants. These facts indicate that *tera askebari* and minibus operators do not always have a fixed superior-subordinate relationship between them, but rather the *tera askebari*'s use of such words can be a tactic to manage minibuses and exercise their power effectively by elevating their status and lowering the addressees' status.

Causative-imperative form

Observation 4: September 2, 2019, 7:50. Western section.

In the morning of September 2, 2019, two vehicles were waiting in the queue in the western section. One minibus barged into the front of the line, asking the *tera askebari*, "*Asgebegn* (አስገበኝ)," which means, "(I ask) can you let me in?" *Tera askebari* YB-A considered the situation and said, "*Bek'a asgebawu* (በቃ አስገባው)," which means, "Well, enough. Let it (the minibus) enter the queue."

Observation 5: September 7, 2019, 17:00. Eastern section.

On September 7, 2019, a number of regular and part-time *tera askebari* stood calculating their earnings in the middle of the road at the eastern part of the terminal. Mgr-B was handing over wages of 200 *birr* to YB-K, who often worked part-time. Meanwhile, one minibus entered the terminal and tried to collect passengers without queuing up. YB-C, who was talking with Mgr-B and YB-K, addressed the minibus operator saying, "*Aswut'awu eski* (አስወጣው እስኪ)," which meant, "Let it (your vehicle) out."

The utterances of two *tera askebari* above consisted of causative grammatical forms as well as imperative. The causative form is expressed by prefix *as-*, indicating that the speaker is allowing someone (indirect object) to perform an action (Appleyard 1995: 245). YB-A's utterance was a type of command to the addressee (minibus driver or attendant) to get (*asgeba-*) the vehicle (*-wu*) into the queue. YB-C's utterance was also a type of command to the minibus operator to get (*aswuta-*) the vehicle (*-wu*) out of the terminal.[11] In the above cases, the *tera askebari*'s use of causative-imperative language indicated that they commanded the minibus workers to carry out certain activities related to handling the vehicles. However, unlike the former cases where the objective form *-wu* was used, the operator here used the suffix *-gn*, which was an objective form in first-person singular (me). Thus, "*asgebegn*" implies a minibus operator's request to the *tera askebari* to permit him to operate. When they depart, they often use jussive forms such as "*ennehid* (እንሂድ)," which means "let us (vehicles) go," to the *tera askebari*, asking permission for departure.

Tera askebari's practice in handling the passengers

Tera askebari help passengers in various ways. First, they assist passengers in boarding minibuses. When passengers ask them about the destination, they indicate the direction by saying, "*Ezih new*" (እዚህ ነው, here) or "*Ezah new*" (እዛ ነው, there). If the platform is located across the street, they say, "*teshegero*" (ተሽገሮ)," which means "(it is located) across the street." They also guide passengers in taking the minibuses. When passengers ask *tera askebari* whether they can enter, they allow it by saying, "*geba/gebi/gebu*" (ግባ/ግቢ/ግቡ, enter).[12] If the minibus is not the appropriate one (such as one that committed some offence), the *tera askebari* say "*ategeba*" (አትግባ, don't enter), and then indicate the specific vehicle by saying "*yeh/yehe*" (ይህ/ይኸ, this) or "*yalessu*" (ያ/አሱ, that). They sometimes specifically indicate the position by saying, "*gebina geba*" (ገቢና ግባ), which means "get in the front passenger seat," or "*kehwala geba*" (ከኋላ ግባ), which means "get in the back seat."

Their activities are not confined to just lining up passengers but extend to social activities too. Very often, *tera askebari* give priority to those with some social disadvantage, such as people with babies, pregnant women, and senior citizens. There seems to be wide consensus among Ethiopians that the socially disadvantaged should be given priority. Those who consider themselves socially weak come to the front and wait for the *tera askebari*'s guidance. Those in the queue also understand that social disadvantage gets priority in the queue. In view of this consensus, *tera askebari* consider social weakness as valid reason for priority. For example, on September 3, 2019, *tera askebari* YB-A shouted *"leju allu! leju allu!"* (ልጅ አሉ! ልጅ አሉ! There are babies!), and stopped the queuers from boarding the vehicle. He first allowed the people with babies to enter the vehicle. One *tera askebari* said, *"chuche ale"* (ጨጨም አለ, there is baby), telling the people that they would give priority to women coming with young babies (October 12, 2019, western section). Furthermore, *tera askebari* often helped passengers who come with heavy luggage (Figure 40). The *tera askebari*'s practice of helping passengers is not aimed at economic profit, but forms part of their social obligation as members of the society.

Figure 40. *Tera askebari* helping passengers to load luggage on the top of the vehicle

Passenger's perception towards *tera askebari*

I conducted 13 interviews with passengers from this terminal. The interviewees were randomly chosen. I asked them several questions on the role of *tera askebari* and satisfaction with their services. The 13 respondents comprised 7 males and 6 females. Their age varied from teenage to the 50s (Table 20). When I asked them about the role of *tera askebari*, most of their answers were related to maintaining the queue. Here, 'Pa' is used as an abbreviation of 'passenger.'

Table 20. List of interview respondents

ID	Age	Gender	Occupation
A	40	Female	Private company worker
B	28	Male	Broker
C	25	Male	Shop manager
D	25	Female	Student
E	17	Female	Student
F	26	Male	Taxi driver
G	52	Male	Businessman
H	15	Male	Student
I	29	Female	Hairdresser
J	32	Female	Civil servant
K	46	Male	Taxi driver
L	38	Female	Graduate school student
M	32	Male	Private company officer

· Pa-H (15, male): "They are making the queue for the passengers" (September 12, 17:28).

· Pa-C (25, male): "They observe whether taxi collects passengers in other place besides the queue" (August 16, 16:44).

· Pa-K (46, male): "They keep the order of the passengers and queuers, let people to enter the vehicles turn by turn. They have discipline on how to do (queuing) (August 2, 9:03).

· Pa-J (32, female): "They are helping the queue, taking the responsibilities in the terminal and required to work on the road ethically" (October 5, 12:30).

While the respondents' answers differed in some aspects, many of them acknowledged the role of *tera askebari* in maintaining the order of passengers and minibuses. Furthermore, some people expressed their view that the *tera askebari*' lining up activities contributed to the safety of the passengers.

· Pa-A (40, female): "They provide lining up service so that people do not get hurt" (August 9, 15:27).
· Pa-F (29, male): "They maintain the order and also protect the people's safety" (August 5, 11:30).
· Pa-C (25, male): "They also need to prevent the criminals (in the terminal)" (August 16, 16:44).

The role of *tera askebari* seems to be understood not only as queue keepers, but also, in a wider frame, as keepers of citizens' safety, regardless of age. While most of them acknowledged the role of *tera askebari*, some expressed negative opinions about their traits and behaviors.

· Pa-K (46, male): "They have a problem. They do not have a good trait" (August 2, 9:03).
· Pa-L (38, female): "Most of them are not originated from Addis Ababa. They came from rural area and not well educated. Most of them have inferior complex and express it by doing rude behaviors. They use all their money by doing *khat* and drinking alcohol" (August 30, 15:00).
· Pa-M (32, male): "All the *tera askebari* are *duriye* (vagrant). They do not have good characters and attitudes" (September 7, 13:43).

While not many of the people expressed their personal feelings on *tera askebari*, some respondents expressed their negative ideas frankly. These were comparatively high social status than the other respondents, such as taxi drivers, graduate school student, and private company officers. This finding reflected the possibilities that the upper classes in the society have stronger negative perspectives on *tera askebari*.

Interestingly, while male respondents have no complaints about the *tera askebari*' touting, many females expressed their negative opinions about their irregular practices.

· Pa-E (17, female): "They are good but not existing in every place. There are some places that *tera askebari* are not existing" (October 5, 12:49).
· Pa-J (32, female): "They sometimes change the line when minibuses give them some money. Also, they sometimes give priority to their acquaintances" (October 5, 12:30).

Nevertheless, most of the respondents (12 of 13) acknowledged the important roles of *tera askebari* at terminals, saying that it would be a problem if there were no *tera askebari,* even though there was a neutral perspective that the minibus business will not be affected much.

· Pa-F (29, male): "A place where *tera askebari* are not existing, it is not a joke. People will barge in, *geregere belo* (noisy), and tumble down" (August 5, 11:30).
· Pa-E (17, female). "They order very well. Unless we (passengers) need to fight with tough taxi (operators)" (October 5, 12:49).
· Pa-K (46, male): "If the *tera askebari* is not existing in the terminal, people will run and enter (the vehicles). The benefits of the *tera askebari* is this. When *tera askebari* come, they (minibus or people) will line up and get the order by sequence. Currently, one minibus fills 12 passengers. When another taxi comes, they will count the passengers and say "enter". The order they create is this" (August 2, 9:03).
· Pa-H (15, male): "It may be a problem but it may not bring huge impact" (September 12, 17:28).

The interviews showed that passengers had double-sided perceptions about *tera askebari*, that is, both positive and negative perceptions. First, respondents from higher social status groups expressed dominant negative views about *tera askebari* related to their origin and educational background. Second, female groups showed a high tendency to consider the *tera askebari*'s informal and inconsistent management methods negatively. Most of the *tera askebari* are male immigrants with low education, and their immethodical management practices seemed to draw criticism from opposite groups. Nonetheless, the majority of interviewees acknowledged the *tera askebari*'s role and contribution in maintaining order at minibus terminals. The interview showed that despite perceptions on *tera askebari*'s way of conduct was double-sided, their managing activity received credit as important roles in keeping the order in the terminal.

Summary

This chapter aimed to figure out the *tera askebari*'s social role and their contribution to society. There are three findings. First, despite having some flexibilities, *tera askebari* were managing minibuses in certain rules which prioritize the social order. In *medebegna gize*, they reacted differently to expel or charge a higher penalty to the infringers who break the rules. Sometimes, they accept their acquaintances by giving them priority in operating services, but these were not frequently happened as it was risky for their business. In *ayer saat*, *tera askebari*'s major role was to embark passengers rapidly. Meanwhile, there were certain challenges they faced, such as passenger's jams or the delay due to the transport workers. In this situation, *tera askebari* does not prioritize keeping the queue, but respond flexibly and try to devise a better solution according to the situation. Second, the terms and phrases that *tera askebari* use in their practice reflect their role as conductors of the minibuses in the terminal. Their language practices have majorly consisted of imperative mode, which was a tactic to manage and exercise their power effectively to addressees. Third, although some passengers had negative perceptions of the *tera askebari*'s behavior, *tera askebari* were widely recognized for their roles and contribution to society.

This study demonstrated that although *tera askebari*'s activities and perceptions toward them were double-sided, their activities were highly recognized as maintaining the social order in the terminal. Until now, the managerial activities of *tera askebari* have been considered negative, both socially and academically. However, in reality, *tera askebari* have been found to play an important role in urban transport by contributing to social order. The study found that although *tera askebari* showed some degree of flexibility, they played a crucial role in the management of urban transportation. They were major agents in producing and reproducing the order in the terminal through the interaction with minibus workers and passengers, and their activities were a process to shape the social order in the urban transport sector.

Notes

[1] A day with no passengers and bad profit is called *t'olabi k'en* (ጥላቢ ቀን, bad day) in slang.

[2] This name is derived from the name of Yetebaberut gas station. This area was called CMC roundabout as well.

[3] The shortcut was called *akwarach* (አቋራጭ, shortcut). Minibus attendants tout by calling out "Semit *bekwarach* (በቋራጭ, through shortcut)" or "Semit Condominium *bekwarach*," literally indicating that the minibus is going through the short cut.

[4] Teregna literally means a person whose turn is to serve (Kane 1990 vol. 1: 963).

[5] The word "tebareri" derives from the word tebarera, which means to flee in several directions, or be driven away (Kane 1990 vol. 1: 877).

[6] When *tera askebari* expel or chasing the *tebareri*, they often command minibus operators by saying, *hid* (ሂድ, go), *sebiyo* (ሰቢዮ, go in Amharic slang), *zor bel* (ዞር በል, go away) *lash bel* (ላሽ በል, go away in Amharic slang).

[7] *Aba* (አባ) is an abbreviation of *Ababa* (አባባ), an address form that is used to name the honorable senior. Aba was more casual, so it was that used among the minibus workers.

[8] *Ayer saat* (አየር ሰዓት) is also called *wef saat* (ወፍ ሰዓት, time of bird). Among minibus workers, passengers are called *wef* (ወፍ), which literally means "a bird" in Amharic. So, a situation of having a number of passengers is called *wef saat*, while having a small number of passengers is called *wef yelem* (ወፍ የለም, no bird) or *ayer yelem* (አየር የለም, no flow).

[9] As *t'aga bel* literally means to narrow the gap, minibus attendants often used this term to ask passengers to sit closer to each other in order to take in more passengers.

[10] The *tera askebari* said that some operators chew khat and become high in the afternoon. This is called *ayre* (አይሬ), *yechat saat* (የጫት ሰዓት), or *yearara saat* (የአራራ ሰዓት). They said that minibus attendants who are in ayre often tout violently.

[11] The other kind of causative-imperative form that the *tera askebari* used is *asmola* (አስሞላ), "Let it (the vehicles) be filled with passengers."

[12] Amharic language has two genders: masculine and feminine. Terms *geba/gebi/gebu* are imperative words meaning "get in" respectively in masculine/feminine/plural forms, respectively. The term *gebu* is also used for

elders to indicate respect. Hereafter, I use only the masculine form.

Chapter 7. Discussion and Conclusion

Informal workers' high adaptability and viability to cope with volatile labor market

With rapid city development, the working population has grown unprecedentedly, and getting a job has become increasingly difficult in urban Africa. In a situation not including unskilled labor in the city's labor market, migrant youths face difficulties in finding job opportunities in the formal sector. While the government did not provide a clear solution, urban youth needed to take measures to survive, which led to involvement in the informal economy. The YBs, who migrated from rural areas, faced various economic and social difficulties. As they do not have professional skills and educational training to find a formal job, they were sustaining their livelihoods by relying on the informal market. However, their employment was insecure due to various informal factors such as verbal contract and unequal relationship with their boss.

For the migrated youths who are finding it difficult to get a stable working chance, affiliating with the Terminal Community was their strategies of survival. First, there was access to communicate with *wanna* and manager, and this gave them a chance to work as a *tera askebari*. Second, the social environment of the terminal provided them an easy access to communicate with drivers and this helped them to expand the work opportunities of minibus attendants and *lamera*, which provided them a high survivability. Lastly, the similarities of transport work have become merit for them to keep coming to the Terminal Community. Instead of transferring to other work in a different profession, which takes time and effort, the YBs could choose similar kinds of works in the terminal, which was easy to learn and had easier job mobility.

The YBs showed great learning abilities to change their occupation rapidly, were strategically seeking opportunities, and easily adapted to different kinds of work. Previous research has observed transport workers as precarious, treating them passively, who were easily affected by external forces. However, the YB's strategies to maintain connection with the Terminal Community and their attitudes and activities to acquire and transfer to different kinds of opportunities clearly indicate that they are neither precarious nor vulnerable. They were subjective entities who have the power to lead their own lives and who can lay out suitable strategies to cope with the unstable informal labor market.

Transport workers' vital roles in African urban transport

For a long time, transport workers in Africa have been portrayed negatively socially as well as academically. Accounts of analysis explained the violent and notorious nature of African transport is caused by workers' personal characteristics or their personal background. The pervasive negative view of transport workers impeded understanding their ability and crucial roles that they supply in the aspect of public service, which made it difficult to understand their potential. This was the same case for the *tera askebari*. Notwithstanding their crucial role, their activities have been frowned upon as being unmethodical, and attempts to determine their role and contribution in society have not been achieved.

This thesis provides insight that transport workers play a significant role and contribute to maintaining the social order on the ground. *Tera askebari* actively communicated with minibus workers, passengers, and public servants and tried to make the best choice at each moment. At *medebegna gize*, their major role was to keep the queue of the minibuses, while it was to embark passengers faster at the *ayer saat*. They sometimes deviated from the rules and customs that they created and acted flexibly; but they devised various methods to handle the variable environment of urban transport. Also, their usage of imperative forms was the tactic to manage effectively. Their daily activities do not end at the micro level but continues to the macro level that forms the traffic order of the city. The vacancy of public service on the urban transport led the private operators like *tera askebari* embarked the new way of transport management and the government's indifference perpetuated this system as a core service. Despite some level of flexibility, *tera askebari* interact with the citizens and try to devise the best solution in each situation. Currently, their activities were widely recognized as important among the citizens. The *tera askebari*'s case indicates that transport workers are major agents in producing and reproducing the public order on the ground, which was a process to shape the social order in the urban transport sector.

Tera askebari as *balemuya*

The development in urban Africa is changing societies rapidly and these conditions are posing certain challenges to urban residents, especially those who depend their lives on the informal economy. Under these circumstances, the strategy that *tera askebari* layout was to weave the networks of formality and informality.

Tera askebari was a form of legal microenterprises controlling transport, in which the legal operators and informal workers were co-existing. Despite their groups being registered as formal enterprises, *tera askebari*'s activities were rather closed to "informal," which manages transport with their own standards without state control. The *wanna tera askebari* (boss) were developed from the street gangs starting from the 1980s and gained a formal license in 2011. Under the low government intervention, the *wanna* were utilized the MSEs regulation and earned high benefits by subcontracting the daily workers informally. Meanwhile, YBs, contract workers, who did not get benefit from both government policy and *wanna*'s employment, were rather utilizing this system as a platform to expand their working opportunities. Although *wanna* earned benefits through the system that they constructed, it was a space for the urban youth to participate in labor activities and earn higher earnings than the other jobs.

While the city government could not make outstanding results on the involvement of *tera askebari* and failed to embrace the burgeoning youth into the labor market, it was *tera askebari* who were actively working and creating various opportunities on the ground. They were the main actors who subjectively layout their livelihoods in urban transport and shape the order of Addis Ababa. In this manner, I argue that "informality" in African transport, which had been largely understood as a realm that caused by the failure or state policy and a state of disorder, should be understood as a process of transport workers' major platform to participate, earn a living, interact with the society, and shape a social order.

Tera askebari are dragging and weaving the networks of formality and informality, and this enhanced their chances of survival. This reveals that the urban youths are cleverly utilizing the concept of in/formal to make their lives in urban Addis Ababa. They are smart and strategic enough to cope up with the variable environment and possess high survivability to deal with the future shock. In the previous part of the thesis, I mentioned that *balemuya* refers to a person who is skilled and proficient in a certain field or activity. I argue that *tera askebari* are *balemuya*, smart strategists, who cleverly utilize the complex mixture of in/formality and shape the dynamic features of urban transport in the center of Addis Ababa.

References

Aalen, L. 2011. *The Politics of Ethnicity in Ethiopia: Actors, Power and Mobilisation under Ethnic Federalism*. Leiden: Brill.

Aalen, L. & K. Tronvoll. 2009. The End of Democracy? Curtailing Political and Civil Rights in Ethiopia, *Review of African Political Economy* 120: 193-207.

Abbink, J. 1998. Briefing: The Eritrean-Ethiopian Border Dispute, *African Affairs* 97(389): 551-565.

_____. 2000. The Organization and Observation of Elections in Federal Ethiopia: Retrospect and Prospect. In Abbink, J. & G. Hesseling eds., *Election Observation and Democratization in Africa*. London: Palgrave Macmillan, pp. 150-179.

_____. 2006. Discomfiture of Democracy? The 2005 Election Crisis in Ethiopia and Its Aftermath, *African Affairs* 105(419): 173-199.

Addis Ababa Chamber of Commerce and Sectoral Associations (AACCSA). 2009. *The Management of Commercial Road Transport in Ethiopia*. Addis Ababa: AACCSA. <https://ethiopianchamber.com/Data/Sites/1/psd-hub-publications/the-management-of -commercial-road-transport-in-ethiopia.pdf> (Accessed on September 15, 2021)

Addis Ababa City Administration (AACA). 2011. *Addis Ababa Non-motorized Transport Strategy, 2011-2020*. Addis Ababa: AACA. (Written in Amharic)

Addis Ababa City Planning Project Office (AACPPO). 2017. Addis Ababa City Structure Plan (Draft Final Summary Report, 2017-2027) Addis Ababa: AACPPO. <https://c40-production-images.s3.amazonaws.com/other_uploads/images/2036_Addi s_Ababa_Structural_Plan_2017_to_2027.original.pdf?1544193458 > (Accessed on September 27, 2021)

Addis Ababa Road and Transport Bureau (AARTB). 2012. *Statistics on Number of Vehicles Registered in Addis Ababa by Type between 1993 and 2011*. Addis Ababa: AARTB. (Written in Amharic)

_____. 2019. *Statistics on Routes and Vehicles on Paratransit Transportation in 2019*. Addis Ababa: AARTB. (Written in Amharic)

Addis Ababa Transport Authority (AATA). 2017. *Waiting time to get public transportation service at public transport terminals and survey to identify related problems*. Addis Ababa: AATA.

African Development Bank (AfDB). 2013. *African Economic Outlook: Structural Transformation and Natural Resources*. Tunis: AfDB.

Agbiboa, D.E. 2018. Informal Urban Governance and Predatory Politics in Africa: The Role of Motor-Park Touts in Lagos, *African Affairs* 117(466): 62-82.

_____. 2020. Introduction. In Agbiboa, D.E. ed., *Transport, Transgression and Politics in African Cities*. London: Routledge, pp. 1-16.

Al Sayyad, N. 2004. Urban Informality as a "New" Way of Life. In Roy, A & N. AlSayyad eds., *Urban Informality: Transnational Perspectives from the Middle East, Latin America, and South Asia*. Lanham: Lexington Books, pp. 7-30.

Amegah, A.K. & S. Agyei-Mensah. 2017. Urban Air Pollution in Sub-Saharan Africa: Time for Action, *Environmental Pollution* 220(2017): 738-743.

Andreasen, J. 1990. Urban-Rural Linkages and Their Impact on Urban Housing in Kenya. In Baker, J ed., *Small Town Africa: Studies in Rural-Urban Interaction* (Seminar Proceedings No. 23). Uppsala: e Scandinavian Institute of African Studies, pp. 161-171.

Andreasen, M.H. & L. Møller-Jensen. 2016. Beyond the Networks: Self-Help Services and Post-Settlement Network Extensions in the Periphery of Dar es Salaam, *Habitat International* 53: 39-47.

Andrews, D., A.C. Sánchez & Å. Johansson. 2011. *Towards Better Understanding of the Informal Economy* (OECD Economics Department Working Papers No. 873). Paris: Organisation for Economic Co-operation and Development.

Appleyard, D. 1995. *Colloquial Amharic: A Complete Language Course*. Routledge: New York.

Arega Seyoum, Muhammed Aragie & Daniel Tadesse. 2016. Growth of Micro and Small Enterprises in Addis Ababa City Administration: A Study on Selected Micro and Small Enterprise in Bole Sub City, *International Journal of Scientific and Research Publications* 6(1): 581-592.

Balsvik, R.R. 2007. *The Quest for Expression: State and the University in Ethiopia under Three Regimes, 1952-2005*. Addis Ababa: Addis Ababa University Press.

Banchialem, A. 2017. *Ethiopia-AFRICA-P151819-Ethiopia: Transport Systems Improvement Project (TRANSIP) Procurement Plan (No. STEP23497)*. Washington, DC: World Bank.

Bank, L. 1991. A Culture of Violence: The Migrant Taxi Trade in QwaQwa, 1980-90. In Preston-Whyte, E. & C. Rogerson eds., *South Africa's Informal Economy*. Cape Town: Oxford University Press, pp. 124-141.

Bauman, Z. 2004. *Wasted Lives: Modernity and Its Outcasts*. Hoboken: John Wiley & Sons.

Bayat, A. 2004. Globalization and the Politics of the Informals in the Global South. In Roy, A. & N. Al Sayyad eds., *Urban Informality: Transnational Perspectives from the Middle East, Latin America, and South Asia*. Lanham: Lexington Books, pp. 79-104.

Bayou Mulat. 1991. The Commercial Road Transport Sector in Ethiopia: Performance, Problems and Future Prospects. In Mekonen Tadesse ed., *The Ethiopian Economy:*

Structure, Problems and Policy Issues. Addis Ababa: Publisher not identified, pp. 183-193.

Berhanu Woldetensae. 2017. *Sustaining Sustainable Mobility: The Integration of Multimodal Public Transportation in Addis Ababa* (Doctoral Dissertation). Department of History, University of Lyon.

Berihu Assefa, Abebaw Zerfu & Biruk Tekle. 2014. *Identifying Key Success Factors and Constraints in Ethiopia's MSE Development: An Exploratory Research* (Research Report 18). Addis Ababa: Ethiopian Development Research Institute.

Britwum, A.O. & A.D. Akorsu. 2017. Organising Casual Workers on an Oil Palm Plantation in Ghana. In Webster, E., A.O. Britwum & S. Bhowmik eds., *Crossing the Divide: Work and the Future of Labour*. Pietermaritzburg: University of KwaZulu-Natal Press, pp. 33-53.

Bromley, R. 1978. Introduction - The Informal Sector: Why Is It Worth Discussing?, *World Development* 6(1978): 1033-1039.

_____. 2004. Power, Property, and Poverty: Why De Soto's "Mystery of Capital" Cannot Be Solved. In Roy, A & N. AlSayyad eds., *Urban Informality: Transnational Perspectives from the Middle East, Latin America, and South Asia*. Lanham: Lexington Books, pp. 271-288.

Burgoyne, C. 1967. Sequel 1960-63, *Ethiopia Observer* 11(4): 278-311.

Carré, F. 2017. *Applying the Concept of the Informal Economy to Labour Market Changes in Developed Countries: What Can Be Learned* (WIEGO Working Paper No. 36). Manchester: WIEGO.

Carter Center. 2009. Observing the 2005 Ethiopia National Elections (Final Report, December 2009). Atlanta: The Carter Center.

Castells, M. & A. Portes. 1989. World Underneath: The Origins, Dynamics, and Effects of the Informal Economy. In Portes, A., M. Castells & L. Benton eds., *The Informal Economy: Studies in Advanced and Less Developed Countries*. Baltimore: John Hopkins University Press, pp. 11-37.

Central Statistical Agency of Ethiopia (CSA). 2003. *Report on Urban Informal Sector, Sample Survey*. Addis Ababa: CSA. (Written in Amharic)

_____. 2005. *Report on Biannual Employment and Unemployment Survey* (Statistical Bulletin 301). Addis Ababa: CSA. (Written in Amharic)

_____. 2007. *The 2007 Population and Housing Census of Ethiopia*. Addis Ababa: CSA.

Chae, H. 2015. A Study on Informality as a Practice of Urban Space Formation. *Anthropia* 1: 105-126. (Written in Korean)

Chinigò, D. 2019. 'The Peri-Urban Space at Work': Micro and Small Enterprises,

Collective Participation, and the Developmental State in Ethiopia, *Africa* 89(1): 79-99.

Choi, S. & S. Jeong. 2011. *The Minimum Housing Standard for Shared Housing Supply* (KRIHS 18-08). Sejong: Korea Research Institute for Human Settlements. (Written in Korean)

Colletta, N.J., M. Kostner & I. Wiederhofer. 1996. *Case Studies in War-to-Peace Transition: The Demobilization and Reintegration of Ex-Combatants in Ethiopia, Namibia, and Uganda* (Vol. 331). Herndon: The World Bank Publications.

Davison Muchadenyika. 2019. Informal Transport, Politics and Power in Harare. In Agbiboa, D.E. ed., *Transport, Transgression and Politics in African Cities: The Rhythm and Chaos*. New York: Routledge, pp. 60-77.

De Soto, H. 1989. *The Other Path: The Invisible Revolution in the Third World*. Abbott, J (Trans). New York: Harper and Row.

_____. 2001. Dead Capital and the Poor, *Sais Review* 21(1): 13-43.

Di Nunzio, M. 2012. "We Are Good at Surviving": Street Hustling in Addis Ababa's Inner City, *Urban Forum* 23: 433-447.

_____. 2014. Thugs, Spies and Vigilantes: Community Policing and Street Politics in Inner City Addis Ababa, *Africa* 84(3): 444-465.

_____. 2019. *The Act of Living: Street Life, Marginality, and Development in Urban Ethiopia*. New York: Cornell University Press.

Doherty, J. 2017. Life (and Limb) in the Fast-Lane: Disposable People as Infrastructure in Kampala's Boda Boda Industry, *Critical African Studies* 9(2): 192-209.

Elias Yitbarek. 2018. Addis Ababa: A Collage of Cities. In Elias Yitbarek & L. Stark eds., *The Transformation of Addis Ababa: A Multiform African City*. Newcastle upon Tyne: Cambridge Scholars, pp. 21-76.

Emmanuel Imaniranzi. 2015. *The Response of Other Drivers to Minibus Taxi Drivers' On-Road Aggressive Behavior: A Case Study in Cape Town, South Africa* (Master's Thesis). Faculty of Engineering, Stellenbosch University.

Eshetie Berhan, Birhanu Beshah & Daniel Kitaw. 2013. Performance Analysis on Public Bus Transport of the City of Addis Ababa, *International Journal of Computer Information Systems and Industrial Management Applications* 5(2150-7988): 722-728.

Eyob Balcha. 2009. *Youth and Politics in Post 1974 Ethiopia: Intergenerational Analysis* (Master's Thesis). International Institute of Social Studies, Erasmus University Rotterdam.

Fekadu Kassa. 2013. Roles of Informal Bus Operators in the City of Addis Ababa, Ethiopia, *Urban Transport Journal* 12(1): 63-73.

_____. 2014. Informal Transport and Its Effects in the Developing World: A Case Study of Addis Ababa, *Journal of Transport Literature* 8(2): 113-133.

Frehiwot Negatu. 2013. *The Impact of Taxi Zoning on Service Delivery the Case of Yeka* (Master's Thesis). Geography and Environmental Studies, Addis Ababa University.

Gemechu Ayana & B. Reilly. 2011. Access to Credit and Informality among Micro and Small Enterprises in Ethiopia, *International Review of Applied Economics* 25(3): 313-329.

Gibbs, T. 2014. Becoming a "Big Man" in Neo-Liberal South Africa: Migrant Masculinities in the Minibus-Taxi Industry, *African Affairs* 113(452): 431-448.

Gilkes, P. 2003. National Identity and Historical Mythology in Eritrea and Somaliland, *Northeast African Studies* 10(3): 163-187.

Glaser, C. 2000. *Bo-Tsotsi: The Youth Gangs of Soweto, 1935-1976*. London: James Currey.

Gleave, G., A. Marsden, T. Powell, S. Coetze, G. Fletcher, I. Barret & D. Storer. 2005. *A Study of Institutional, Financial and Regulatory Frameworks of Urban Transport in Large Sub-Saharan African Cities* (SSATP Working Paper 82). Washington, DC: World Bank.

Graziano, A.A. 2014. *The Use of the Car Rapide as a Living Symbol of Senegal* (Independent Study Project Collection). Nashville: SIT Study Abroad.

Habtai Zerai. 1987. *A Historical Development of the Town of Kombolcha, 1937-1974* (Senior Essay). Department of History, Addis Ababa University.

Hansen, K.T. 2015. Cities of Youth: Post-Millennial Cases of Mobility and Sociality. In Resnick, D. & J. Thurlow eds., *African Youth and the Persistence of Marginalization*. New York: Routledge, pp. 67-84.

Harper, M. & G. Finnegan. 1998. *Value for Money? Impact of Small Enterprise Development*. London: Intermediate Technology Publications.

Harper, M. 2000. *Public Services through Private Enterprise: Micro-Privatisation for Improved Delivery*. London: Intermediate Technology Publications.

Hart, J. 2016. *Ghana on the Go: African Mobility in the Age of Motor Transportation*. Indiana University Press.

Hart, K. 1973. Informal Income Opportunities and Urban Employment in Ghana, *The Journal of Modern African Studies* 11(1): 61-89.

Heinonen, P. 2011. *Youth Gangs and Street Children Culture, Nurture and Masculinity in Ethiopia* (Social Identities, Vol. 7). New York: Berghahn Books.

Howe, J. & D. Bryceson. 2000. *Poverty and Urban Transport in East Africa: Review of Research and Dutch Donor Experience* (A Report Prepared for the World Bank). Washington, DC: World Bank.

Independent Evaluation Group (IEG). 2008. *ICR Review* (Report No. ICRR 12919). http://documents1.worldbank.org/curated/en/541551474481168177/text/000020051-2 0140619073524.txt (Accessed on November 8, 2021)

International Labour Organization (ILO) 1972. *Employment, Incomes and Equality: A Strategy for Increasing Productive Employment in Kenya* (Report of an Inter-Agency Team Financed by the United Nations Development Programme and Organised by the International Labour Office). Geneva: ILO.

_____. 2002. *Decent Work and the Informal Economy: Sixth Item on the Agenda* (Report VI). International Labour Conference 90th Session. Geneva: ILO.

_____. 2018. *Women and Men in the Informal Economy: A Statistical Picture* (Third Edition). Geneva: ILO.

Imam Mahmoud & Yonas Alemayehu. 2018. Experiences of the Poor in the Contemporary Urban Resettlement of Addis Ababa. In Elias Yitbarek & L. Stark eds., *The Transformation of Addis Ababa: A Multiform African City*. Newcastle upon Tyne: Cambridge Scholars, pp. 127-160.

Isaac Ishmael. 2013. *"Streetism": A Socio-Cultural and Pastoral Theological Study of a Youth Problem in Ghana*. Bloomington: Author House.

James Michira. 2018. Language, Resistance and Subversive Identities in the Matatu Sub-Culture, *The International Journal of Humanities and Social Studies* 6(3): 242-253.

Kamau Wango. 2020. 'Matatu' Graffiti as an Avenue for Self-Expression and Social Commentary Among the Youth in Nairobi, Kenya, *East African Journal of Arts and Social Sciences* 2(1): 87-103.

Kane, T.L. 1990. *Amharic-English Dictionary* (Vol. 1 & Vol. 2). Harrassowitz Verlag: Wiesbaden.

Kenda Mutongi. 2006. Thugs or Entrepreneurs? Perceptions of Matatu Operators in Nairobi 1970 to Present, *Africa* 76(4): 549-568.

_____. 2017. *Matatu: A History of Popular Transportation in Nairobi*. Chicago: University of Chicago Press.

Kim, D. & C. Yoon. 2009. A Study on the Establishment of Minimum Housing Standards for the Socially Underprivileged, *Journal of the Korean Housing Association* 20(3): 47-58. (Written in Korean)

Kim, I. & H.V. Milner. 2019. Multinational Corporations and Their Influence through Lobbying on Foreign Policy. In Foley, C.F., J.R. Hines & D. Wessel eds., *Global Goliaths: Multinational Corporations in the 21st Century Economy*. Washington, DC: The Brookings Institution, pp. 497-536.

Klopp, J. & C.M. Cavoli. 2018. The Paratransit Puzzle: Master Planning for

Transportation in Maputo and Nairobi. In Uteng, T.P. & L. Karen eds., *(Im)mobilities in the City-Creating Knowledge for Planning Cities in the Global South and Postcolonial Cities*. New York: Routledge, pp. 95-110.

Kumar, A. & F. Barrett. 2008. *Stuck in Traffic: Urban Transport in Africa* (Africa Infrastructure Country Diagnostic, Summary of Background Paper 1). Washington, DC: World Bank.

La Fontaine, J.S. 1970. Two Types of Youth Group in Kinshasa (Leopoldville). In Mayer, P. ed., *Socialization: The Approach from Social Anthropology*. London: Tavistock, pp. 191-214.

Lee-Smith, D. 1989. Urban Management in Nairobi: A Case Study of the Matatu Mode of Public Transport. In Stren, R.E. & R.R. White eds., *African Cities in Crises: Managing Rapid Urban Growth*. London: Westview Press, pp. 276-304.

Lesetedi, G.N. 2003. Urban-Rural Linkages as an Urban Survival Strategy among Urban Dwellers in Botswana: The Case of Broadhurst Residents, *Journal of Political Ecology* 10(1): 37-46.

Leslau, W. 1973. *English-Amharic Context Dictionary*. Wiesbaden: Otto Harrassowitz Verlag.

Lindell, I. 2010. Introduction: The Changing Politics of Informality - Collective Organizing, Alliances and Scales of Engagement. In Lindell, I. ed., *Africa's Informal Workers: Collective Agency, Alliances and Transnational Organizing in Urban Africa*. London: Zed Books, pp. 1-30.

Lucas, K. 2011. Making the Connections between Transport Disadvantage and the Social Exclusion of Low Income Populations in the Tshwane Region of South Africa, *Journal of Transport Geography* 19(6): 1320-1334.

Lyons, T. 2006. Ethiopia in 2005: The Beginning of Transition? *Africa Notes* (No. 25, January 2006). Washington, DC: Center for Strategic and International Studies.

Macrae, J. 2010. The Life and History of Minibuses, *Ferenge Ethiopia* 24: 5-6.

Makoma Mabilo. 2018. *Women in the Informal Economy: Precarious Labour in South Africa* (Master's Thesis). Faculty of Arts and Social Sciences, Stellenbosch University.

Mariani, G. 1938. Corriere dell' Impero, *La Lotta Contro le Richettsiosi Umane Nell' Africa Orientale Italiana*: 59-60 (Retrieved from Pankhurst, R. 1973).

Markos Kidane, Dugassa Mulugeta, Addis Adera, Yonas Yimmam & Tigabu Molla. 2015. Determinants of Microenterprises Targeting Youth Group in Addis Ababa, Ethiopia, *Journal of World Economic Research* 4(3): 71-82.

Mary Njeri. 2010. *Social Relations and Associations in the Informal Sector in Kenya* (Social Policy and Development Programme Paper No. 43). Geneva: United Nations

Research Institute for Social Development.

Mbugua wa Mungai. 2013. *Nairobi's Matatu Men: Portrait of a Subculture* (Contact Zones NRB TEXT - 07). Nairobi: Goethe-Institut Kenya, Native Intelligence, and the Jomo Kenyatta Foundation.

Mbugua wa Mungai & D.A. Samper. 2006. "No Mercy, No Remorse": Personal Experience Narratives about Public Passenger Transportation in Nairobi, Kenya, *Africa Today* 52(3): 51-81.

Meagher, K. 2010. The Politics of Vulnerability: Exit, Voice and Capture in Three Nigerian Informal Manufacturing Clusters. In Lindell, I. ed., *Africa's Informal Workers: Collective Agency, Alliances and Transnational Organizing*. London: Zed Books, pp. 46-64.

Meaza Cheru. 2016. *Solid Waste Management in Addis Ababa: A New Approach to Improving the Waste Management System* (Bachelor's Thesis). Department of Engineering, Helsinki Metropolia University of Applied Sciences.

Medina, L., A. Jonelis & M. Cangul. 2017. *The Informal Economy in Sub-Saharan Africa: Size and Determinants* (WF/17/156). Washington, DC: International Monetary Fund.

Miller, W.B. 1980. Gangs, Groups, and Serious Youth Crime. In Schicor, D. & D. Kelly eds., *Critical Issues in Juvenile Delinquency*. Lexington, MA: Lexington Books, pp. 115-138.

Ministry of Urban Development & Housing (MUDH). 2016. *Micro and Small Enterprise Development Policy & Strategy* (Second edition). Addis Ababa: Ministry of Urban Development & Housing.

Mintesnot Gebeyehu & S. Takano. 2007. Diagnostic Evaluation of Public Transport Mode Choice in Addis Ababa, *Journal of Public Transportation* 10(4): 27-50.

Mobereola, D. 2009. *Africa's First Bus Rapid Transit Scheme: The Lagos BRT-Lite System* (SSATP Discussion Paper No. 9, Urban Transport Series). Washington, DC: World Bank.

Moser, C. 1998. Reassessing Urban Poverty Reduction Strategies: The Asset Vulnerability Framework, *World Development* 26(1): 1-19.

Nebiyu Baye. 2015. *Politicizing Waste Collection and Discipling Waste Collectors: A Critical Analysis of Waste Management Practice in Addis Ababa, Ethiopia 2003-2012* (Doctoral Dissertation). Department of Philosophy in Planning, University of Toronto.

Negash, T. & L. Tronvoll. 2000. *Brothers at War: Making Sense of the Eritrean-Ethiopian War*. Suffolk: James Currey.

Onchiri Haron. 2010. *Graffiti Perspective on Matatus in Kenya: A Lexico-Pragmatic Theory* (Master's Thesis). Department of Linguistics and Languages, University of

Nairobi.

Palmer, I. & S. Berrisford. 2015. *Urban Infrastructure in Sub-Saharan Africa: Harnessing Land Values, Housing and Transport* (Literature Review on Public Transport Report 4). London: UK Aid.

Pankhurst, E.S. 1958. Road Transport for Passengers and Fright, *Ethiopia Observer* 1(12): 392-393.

Pankhurst, R. 1968. Road Building during the Italian Fascist Occupation of Ethiopia 1936-1941, *African Quarterly* 15(3): 21-63.

_____. 1973. The Medical History of Ethiopia During the Italian Fascist Invasion and Occupation, *Ethiopia Observer* 16(2):108-117.

Pirie, G. 2013. *Sustainable Urban Mobility in 'Anglophone' Sub-Saharan Africa* (Global Report on Human Settlements 2013). Nairobi: UN Habitat.

_____. 2014. Transport Pressures in Urban Africa: Practices, Policies, Perspectives. In Parnell, S. & E. Pieterse eds., *Africa's Urban Revolution*. London: Zed Books, pp. 133-147.

Podestà, G.L. 2013. Building the Empire: Public Works in Italian East Africa (1936-1941), *Entreprises et Historie* 70(1): 37-53.

Portes, A. & R. Schauffler. 1993. Competing Perspectives on the Latin American Informal Sector, *Population and Development Review* 19(1): 33-60.

Portes, A. & W. Haller. 2010. The Informal Economy. In Smelser, J.J. & R. Swedberg eds., *The Handbook of Economic Sociology*. New Jersey: Princeton University Press, pp. 403-425.

Phanuel William. 2016. *Strategy Practice in the Informal Economy: A Case from Strategic Networking of Informal Printing Business in Ghana* (Doctoral Dissertation). Department of Management, Marketing and Entrepreneurship, University of Canterbury, New Zealand.

Rahel Wasihun & Issac Paul. 2010. Growth Determinants of Women-Operated Micro and Small Enterprises in Addis Ababa, *Journal of Sustainable Development in Africa* 12(6): 233-246.

Rakodi, C. & T. Lloyd-Jones. 2002. *Urban Livelihoods: A People-Centred Approach to Reducing Poverty*. Washington, DC: Earthscan Publication.

Rasmussen, J. 2012. Inside the System, Outside the Law: Operating the Matatu Sector in Nairobi. *Urban Forum* 23(4): 415-432.

Richard Tambulasi & Happy Kayuni. 2008. Can the State Perpetuate the Marginalisation of the Poor? The Socio-Economic Effects of the State's Ban on Minibus 'Callboys' in Malawi, *Development Southern Africa* 25(2): 215-226.

Rizzo, M. 2011. 'Life is War': Informal Transport Workers and Neoliberalism in Tanzania

1998-2009, *Development and Change* 42(5): 1179-1205.

_____. 2017. *Taken for a Ride: Grounding Neoliberalism, Precarious Labour, and Public Transport in an African Metropolis*. Oxford: Oxford University Press.

Rizzo, M. & M. Atzeni. 2020. Workers' Power in Resisting Precarity: Comparing Transport Workers in Buenos Aires and Dar es Salaam, *Work, Employment and Society* 34(6): 1114-1130.

Shaw, M. 2002. *Crime and Policing in Post-Apartheid South Africa: Transforming under Fire*. Bloomington: Indiana University Press.

Shelemay Kay. 2009. Music of the Ethiopian American Diaspora: A Preliminary Overview (Seminar Proceedings). In Ege, S., H. Aspen, Birhanu Teferra & Shiferaw Bekele eds., *Proceedings of the 16th International Conference of Ethiopian Studies: July 2-6, 2007*. Wiesbaden: Harrassowitz, pp. 1153-1164.

Siyabulela Fobosi. 2021. Uncovering Precarious Working Conditions in the Global South: A Case of the Minibus Taxi Industry in South Africa, *International Journal of Engineering, Management and Humanities* 2(3): 138-146.

Talbot, D.A. 1952. *Contemporary Ethiopia*. New York: Philosophical Library.

Tilahun Meshesha. 2014. Demands for Urban Public Transportation in Addis Ababa, *Journal of Intelligent Transportation and Urban Planning* 2(3): 121-128.

Tom Odera. 2015. *Boda-Boda Economy: Its Socioeconomic Impact on Rural Bondo* (Bachelor Thesis). Diaconia University of Applied Sciences.

Trebilcock, A. 2005. *Decent Work and the Informal Economy* (WIDER Discussion Paper No. 2005/04). Helsinki: World Institute for Development Economics Research.

Tronvoll, K. 2011. The Ethiopian 2010 Federal and Regional Elections: Re-Establishing the One-Party State, *African affairs* 110(438): 1-16.

Tokman, V.E. 2007. *Modernizing the Informal Sector* (UNDESA Working Paper No. 42). New York: United Nations Department of Economic and Social Affairs.

United Nation Department of Economic and Social Affairs (UNDESA). 2018. *World Urbanization Prospects* (ST/ESA/SER.A/420). New York: United Nations. <https://population.un.org/wpp/Download/Standard/Population/> (Accessed on July 1, 2021)

United Nation Habitat (UN Habitat). 2013. *Planning and Design for Sustainable Urban Mobility* (Global Report on Human Settlements). Abingdon and New York: Routledge.

United Nations International Children's Emergency Fund (UNICEF). 2002. *The State of the World's Children 2002: Leadership*. New York: UNICEF.

Vaughan, S. & K. Tronvoll. 2003. The Culture of Power in Contemporary Ethiopian Political Life. *Sida Studies No.10*. Stockholm: Swedish International Development

Cooperation Agency.

Venter, C., V. Vokolkova & J. Michalek. 2007. Gender, Residential Location, and Household Travel: Empirical Findings from Low-Income Urban Settlements in Durban, South Africa, *Transport Reviews* 27(6): 653-677.

Villancourt-Laflamme, C. 2005. *Trade Unions and Informal Workers' Associations in the Urban Informal Economy of Ecuador* (Working Paper No. 57). Geneva: Policy Integration Department, ILO.

Voukas, Y. & D. Palmer. 2012. Sustainable Transportation in East Africa: The Bus Rapid Transit Evolution in Addis Ababa, Ethiopia (Paper Presentation). *Conference CODATU XV, The Role of Urban Mobility in (Re)Shaping Cities*. Addis Ababa, Ethiopia. <http://www.codatu.org/wp-content/uploads/Y.-Voukas-D.-Palmer-ARTICLE-Codatu-XV-2012-EN.pdf> (Accessed on November 1, 2021)

Williams, C.C., J. Round & R. Peter. 2007. Beyond the Formal/Informal Economy Binary Hierarchy, *International Journal of Social Economics* 34(6): 402-414

Wolday Amha. 2016. Growth of Youth-Owned MSEs in Ethiopia: Characteristics, Determinants and Challenges, *Ethiopian Journal of Economics* 24(2): 93-128.

World Bank. 2007. *158,000 Soldiers Demobilized in Ethiopia* (Report No. 92829). Washington, DC: World Bank. <http://documents.worldbank.org/curated/en/969811468247862422/158-000-soldiers-demobilized-in-Ethiopia> (Accessed on November 1, 2021)

Yared Teshome. 2018. Challenges and Opportunities of Micro and Small Enterprises Strategy in Ethiopia Urban Development: The Case of Ambo Town, Oromia Ethiopia, *SDMIMD Journal of Management* 9(2): 55-64.

Online Materials

· Addis Ababa Youth Association (AAYA). 2021. <http://www.aaya.8m.net/index.html> (Accessed on July 22, 2021)

· AfDB (African Development Bank). March 27, 2013. *Recognizing Africa's Informal Sector*. <https://blogs.afdb.org/afdb-championing-inclusive-growth-across-africa/post/recognizing-africas-informal-sector-11645> (Accessed on November 1, 2021)

· Africa News and Reuters. September 8, 2018. *Nigerian Artists Draw Inspiration from Chaotic Transport System*. <https://www.africanews.com/2018/09/08/nigerian-artists-draw-inspiration-from-chaotic-transport-system/> (Accessed on October 14,

2021)

- Al Jazeera. June 9, 2005. *Dozens Killed in Ethiopian Protest.* <https://www. aljazeera.com/news/2005/6/9/dozens-killed-in-ethiopian-protests> (Accessed on July 21, 2021)

- Ethiopian Business Review. February 15, 2018. *Public Transport in Addis from Crisis through Crisis, into Crisis.* <https://ethiopianbusinessreview.net/index. php/topic/item/597-public-transport-in-addis-from-crisis-through-crisis-into-crisis> (Accessed on July 20, 2019)

- Ethiopian Current Affairs Discussion Forum (ECADF). January 28, 2011. *Addis Ababa Protest 2005.* <https://ecadforum.com/addis-ababa-protest-2005/> (Accessed on July 21, 2021)

- Faria, J. 2022. *Cost of living index in selected cities in Africa as of 2021.* <https://www.statista.com/statistics/1218516/cost-of-living-in-selected-african-cities/ > (Accessed on January 29, 2022)

- Federal Transport Authority (FTA). *Historical Origin.* <www.fta.gov.et> (Written in Amharic, Accessed on February 23, 2020)

- Fikrejesus Amhazion. April 23, 2018. *A Look Back on Eritrea's Historic 1993 Referendum.* <https://www.tesfanews.net/revisiting-eritrea-historic-1993-referendum/> (Accessed on October 3, 2020)

- Glader, P. August 23, 2017. *A Journey into the Underground World of Kenya's Graffiti-Crazed Car Culture.* Forbes. <https://www.forbes.com/sites/berlinschoolofcreativeleadership/2017/08/23/a-journe y-into-the-underground-world-of-kenyas-graffiti-crazed-car-culture/> (Accessed on October 14, 2021)

- Guven, M. & R. Karlen. December 03, 2020. *Supporting Africa's Urban Informal Sector: Coordinated Policies with Social Protection at the Core*, World Bank Blogs. <https://blogs.worldbank.org/africacan/supporting-africas-urban-informal-sector-coor dinated-policies-social-protection-core> (Accessed on April 26, 2021)

- Holloway, B. February 7, 2019. *Dakar's Car Rapides: A Symbol of the Senegalese Capital, Culture Trip.* <https://theculturetrip.com/africa/senegal/articles/dakars-car-rapides-a-symbol-of-the-senegalese-capital/> (Accessed on October 14, 2021)

- Humphreys, A. March 20, 2021. *Rethinking Rights at Work: Notes from Matatu Organising in Nairobi.* Agenda for International Development, March 10, 2021. <https://www.a-id.org/2021/03/10/rethinking-rights-at-work-notes-from-matatu-orga nising-in-nairobi/> (Accessed on April 27, 2021)

- International Organization of Motor Vehicle Manufacturers (OICA). 2021.

Statistics on World Vehicles in Use by Country and Type, 2005 to 2015. <http://www.oica.net/category/vehicles-in-use/> (Accessed on July 1, 2021)

- NAMATI. 2021. *Addis Ababa Youth Association.* <https://namati.org/network/ organization/addis-ababa-youth-association/> (Accessed on July 22, 2021)

- Nita Bhalla. May 8, 2001. *Cleaning up the Streets of Addis.* <http://news.bbc.co.uk/2/hi/africa/1319359.stm> (Accessed on October 1, 2021)

- The New York Times. June 7, 2005. *Ethiopian Students and Police Clash Over Disputed Election Results.* <https://www.nytimes.com/2005/06/07/world/africa/ ethiopian-students-and-police-clash-over-disputed-election.html> (Accessed on July 20, 2021)

- WageIndicator.org. 2022. *Archive- Living Wage Series – Ethiopia – September 2019 – In ETB, per Month.* <https://wageindicator.org/salary/living-wage/archive-no-index/ethiopia-living-wage-series-september-2019> (Accessed on January 30, 2022)

- World Bank. 2021. *GDP Growth Annual: Ethiopia.* <https://data.worldbank.org/ indicator/NY.GDP.MKTP.KD.ZG?end=2018&locations=ET&start=2009   (Accessed on July 1, 2021)

- World Bank. 2022a. *Statistics.* <https://data.worldbank.org/indicator/SP.POP. TOTL?locations=ET> (Accessed on January 24, 2022)

- World Bank. 2022b. *Inflation, Consumer Prices (annual %) – Ethiopia.* <https://data.worldbank.org/indicator/FP.CPI.TOTL.ZG?end=2019&locations=ET&s tart=2011&view=chart> (Accessed on January 29, 2022)

- World Bank. 2022c. *Inflation, Consumer Prices (annual %) – World.* <https://data.worldbank.org/indicator/FP.CPI.TOTL.ZG?end=2019&start=2011> (Accessed on January 29, 2022)

- 2Markato.com. December 17, 2021. Ethiopia: Addis Revises Taxi Tariff. <https://www.2merkato.com/news/alerts/6357-ethiopia-addis-revises-taxi-tariff> (Accessed on February 2, 2022)

Acknowledgement

"A Korean lady who studies Ethiopia in Japan." This sentence represents me and explains that I would not have been able to achieve this goal without a support and assistance from countless people from communities that I had belonged it, and currently belonging in.

First and foremost, I would first like to send my earnest gratitude to my major supervisor, Masayoshi Shigeta. Amidst his busy schedule, he allowed his time to have discussions, and his insightful feedback pushed me to sharpen my thinking and brought my work to a higher level. He encouraged me and believed in my potential during and after writing my Ph. D. thesis. I would like to express my sincere appreciation for Professor Morie Kaneko for her dedicated involvement in every step throughout the process of my studies as well as my personal life in a foreign land. She was the one who gladly assisted me whenever I had a personal or academic problem. Also, I would like to send my deepest appreciation to Professor Motoki Takahashi and Professor Misa Hirano-Nomoto for their thoughtful feedback and caring attention to my research, which have been encouraged me throughout my academic journey in Japan. I also would like to give the warmest thanks to professors, staffs, and colleagues in Graduate School of Asian and African Area Studies as well as Division of African Area Studies in Kyoto University.

This book would not be achieved without financial supports from two institutions, KIEP and COSER office of Kyoto University. Through the support from Korea Institute for International Economic Policy (KIEP) with related to the Graduate Program for Area Studies of Hankuk University of Foreign Studies (HUFS), I was able to conduct two-times of field research in 2017 and 2018. The third time's research was supported by Center of On-site Education and Research (COSER) office of Kyoto University, through a project of International On-site Education Program (IOSEP) for Global Human Resources. Also, this study was supported by the Support for Pioneering Research Initiated by the Next Generation program operated by the Japan Science and Technology Agency (JST), JST Spring, grant number JPMJSP2110 and JSPS Scientific Research Fund-B: No.18H03444 and Grant-in-Aid for Transformative Research Areas(A): No.20H05806.

I also send my acknowledgement to professors at Graduate School of International Area Studies and Department of African Studies of Hankuk

University of Korea, especially Myeongsik Kwon, Taesang Chang, Yongkyu Chang, Jeongkyeong Park, Kyudeug Hwang, Haksu Kim, Gwangsu Kim, and Chuljoon Yang, who sustained my interests in Africa up to the current moment. I would also like to acknowledge Young Asian Africanist networks from 2018 to 2023 which was a network between HUFS in Korea, Kyoto University and Ritsumeikan in Japan, Jawaharlal Nehru University in India, and Bayreuth University in Germany, which was an extraordinary experience to share the knowledges and construct the network with young scholars from various countries.

I would like to convey my sincere gratitude to my esteemed and respectable people, whom I respect and communicate like parents and received various supports. My parents in Ethiopia, Mr. Ababa Tesfaye and Mrs. Mama Lubaba, their love and support has been always giving me the power to sustain my work. I would also like to express my sincere thanks to Mr. Joongsan Ahn, professor Yongung Lee, and Mr. Mesfin Mideksa, and his excellency Mr. Il Park a Korean Ambassador to Lebanon, for cheering my future with their heart.

I would like to acknowledge my heartfelt appreciation to my colleagues in Japan and Korea, Kyeri Kim, Nobuko Yamazaki, Kazuki Mitsushima, Seong Eun Park, Otani Takuma, Ryutaro Tara, and Teruya Maehata for giving me productive feedback and inspiring discussions which profoundly helped to develop my research. Also, I send my thanks with affection to my Ethiopian friends and informants who helped me unconditionally when I was at field, Tesfaye Demissie, Martina Jordi Anchello, Haile Gezae, Yohana Tesfaye, and Natanael Fekadu.

I want to express my deepest love to my family members for their unwavering supports, my grandmother, Minsu Kwak, my mother, Gyeongim Kim, my father, Chanhwa Choi, and my younger brother Seongjun Choi, and my lovely birds. They kept me going on and this work would not have been possible without their devoted support. Especially, I would like to recall the memories with Chunhee Kim, my maternal grandfather, who is a person who first linked me with Japan. When I was young, he often told me about his experience with the Japanese people and taught me some basic words. Although it was a short moment, the time that we spent was one of the most enjoyable memories in my life. I hope he would be proud of me, smiling at the heaven, that his granddaughter made her journey in his beloved country.

Last but not least, I would like to acknowledge the contribution of all *tera askebari* in Addis Ababa, who are working and moving the city at this very moment.

Publication of the Kyoto University Africa Studies Research Series

The Center for African Area Studies at Kyoto University is a research institution whose precursor was founded in 1986 as the first comprehensive research institution covering Africa. Since its establishment, the institution has been known as the Africa Center, a base for academic research into the African region. Contemporary Africa is currently undergoing significant change in all aspects, be they environmental, social, cultural, political, or economic. It is through that the status of Africa and the role it plays on the world stage will become increasingly important in the future. We are in an era where we have to question fundamentally Africa's characteristics on multiple forms, and we should look toward Africa and understand it as a place inhabited by those of the same era as ourselves as we continue to study it. With this desire at heart, Kyoto University continues to produce young scholars researching Africa. This series aims to present the wider public with the rigorous fieldwork and groundbreaking analysis being conducted by a new wave of ambitious young researchers and was initiated with the support of the 2010 Kyoto University President's Discretionary Fund (Assistance to Publish Young Research) to mark the 25th anniversary of the establishment of the Africa Center.

February 2011
The Center for African Area Studies, Kyoto University

Eunji Choi

EunJI Choi is a researcher at the Center for African Area Studies, Kyoto University, Japan. Born in 1994 in Chuncheon, Republic of Korea, she studied Swahili and Eastern African culture at Hankuk University of Foreign Studies (Bachelor of Arts, 2016). Attracted by the story of thousands of Ethiopians fighting in her hometown during the Korean War, she decided to focus her research on Ethiopia. Since her Master's course, her major research interest was the life strategy of African urbanites in a situation where both formal and informal aspects coexist, which led her to conduct ethnographic research on *tera askebari*, queue keepers at minibus terminals in Addis Ababa (Master of Arts in Anthropology, 2019, Doctor of Area Studies, 2022).

As the first Korean female researcher conducting urban ethnographic research in Ethiopia, she was awarded the Best Presentation Award at the Japan Association of Nilo-Ethiopian Studies for consecutive years in 2019 and 2020. In 2012, she received a research incentive grant, which is sponsored by Support for Pioneering Research operated by the Japan Science and Technology Agency (JPMJSP2110). Her interest was not only in research but in Amharic as well, which led her to work as an Amharic lecturer at Korea National Diplomatic Academy in 2014 and 2015 for diplomats assigned to the Korean Embassy in Ethiopia. Also, she has been working as an Amharic interpreter at Seoul and Gyeongju International Marathon 6 times since 2015.

京都大学アフリカ研究シリーズ 031

Tera Askebari:
Ethnography of Transport Workers in Addis Ababa

2023 年 5 月 31 日 初版発行
著者 Eunji Choi
発行者 松香堂書店
発行所 京都大学アフリカ地域研究資料センター
〒606-8501 京都市左京区吉田下阿達町46
TEL：075-753-7800
Email：caas@jambo.africa.kyoto-u.ac.jp